I0505093

Horse unicorn coloring book for kids ages 4-8

CARLOS MENDEZ

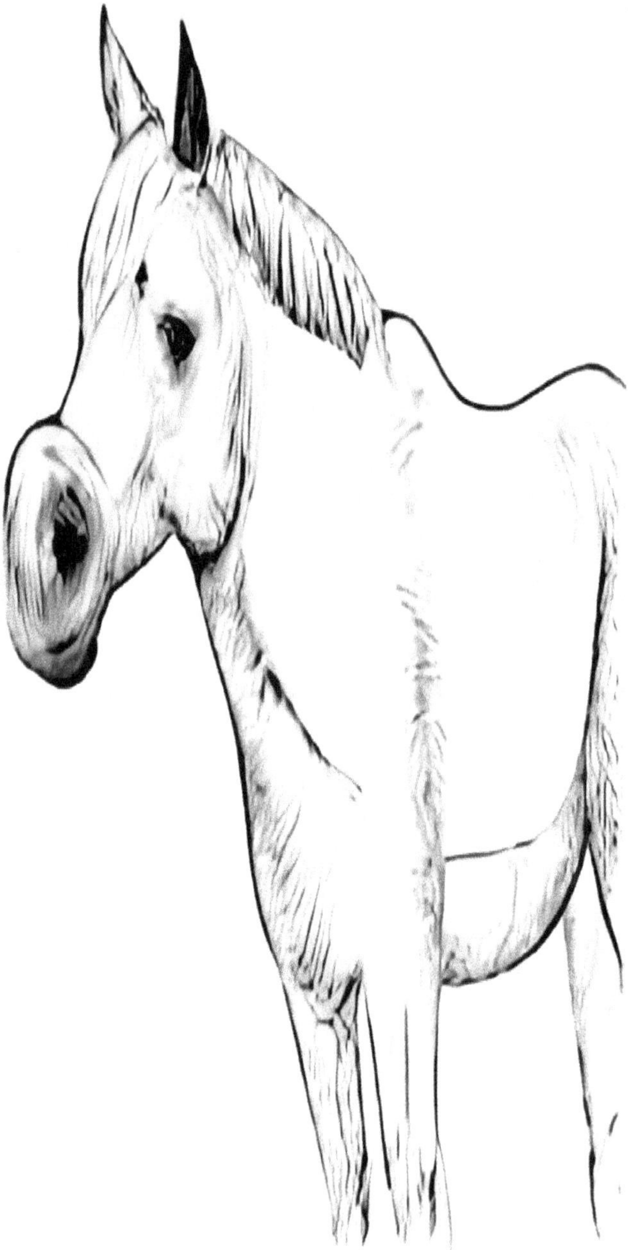

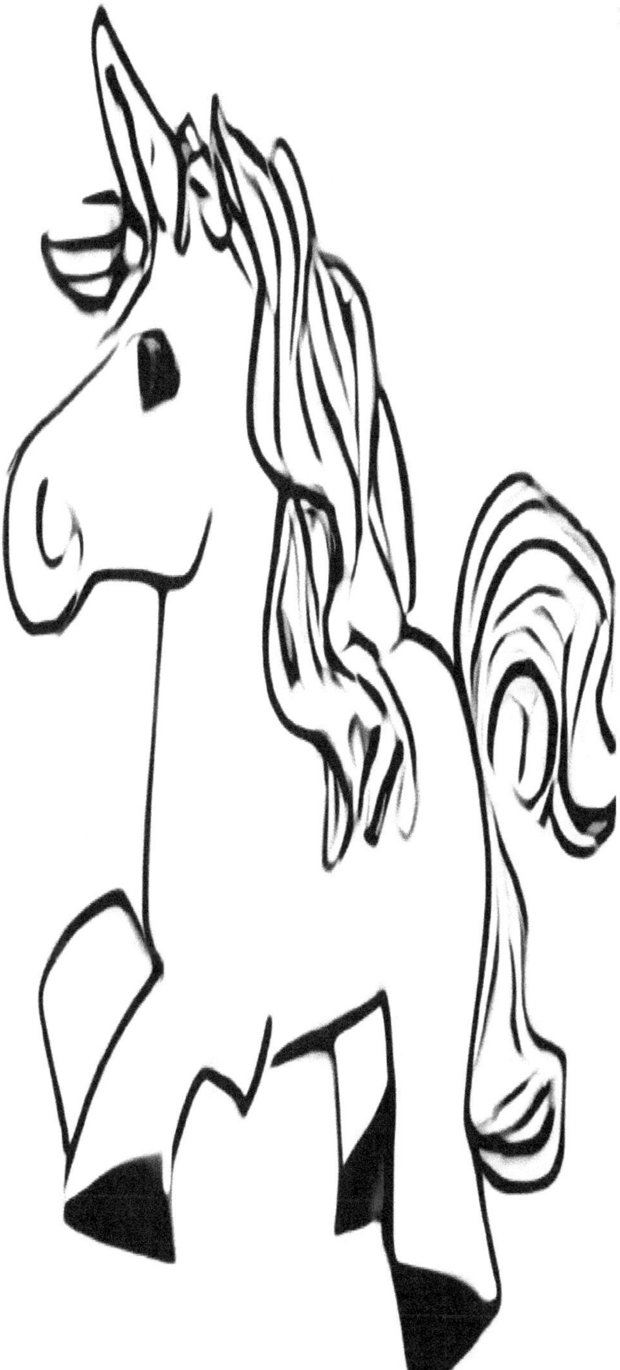

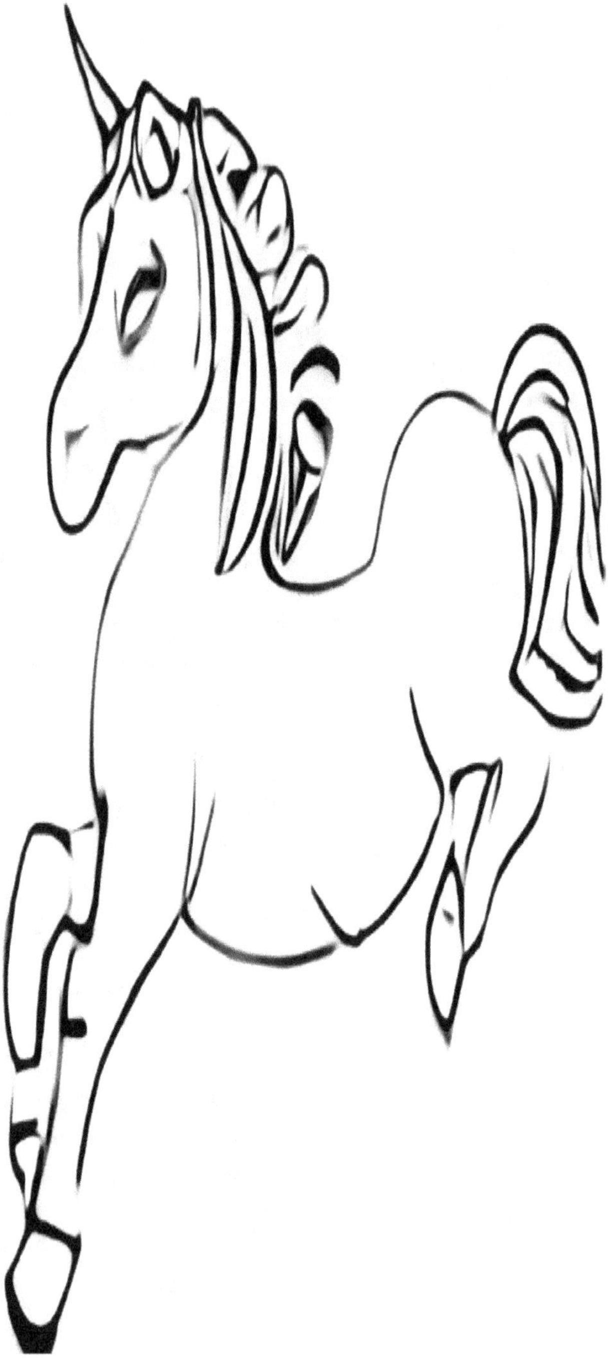

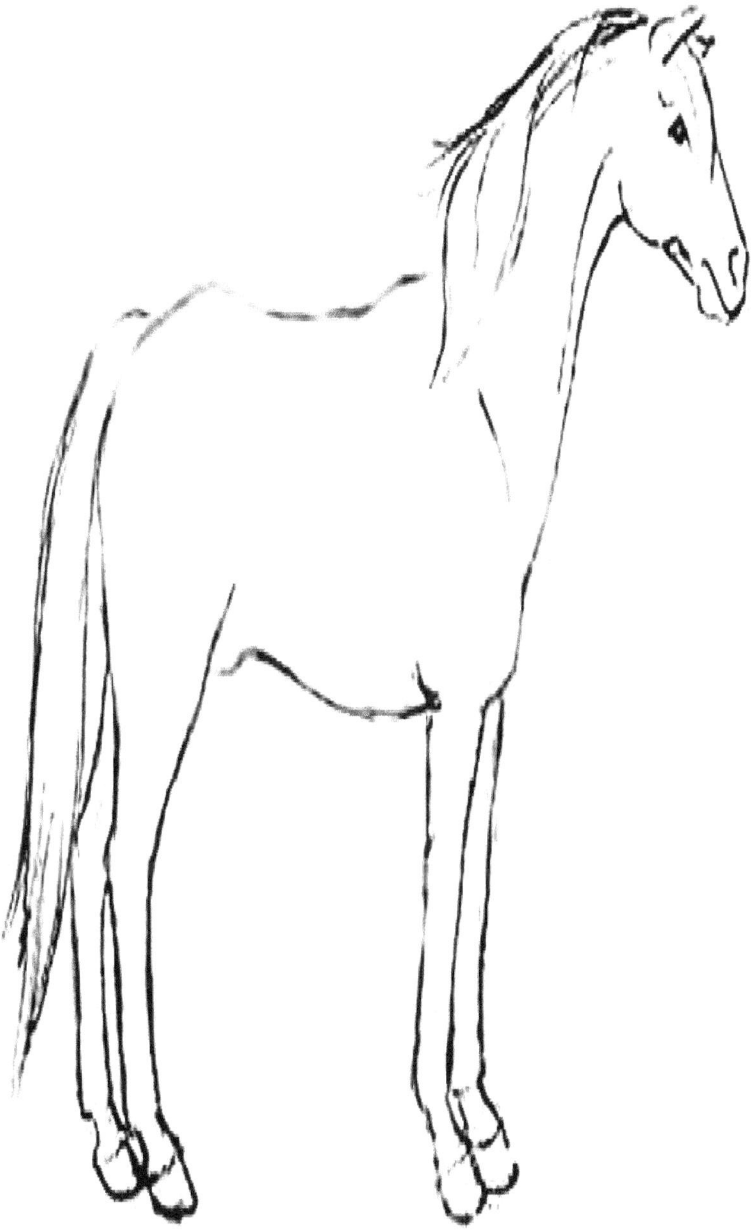

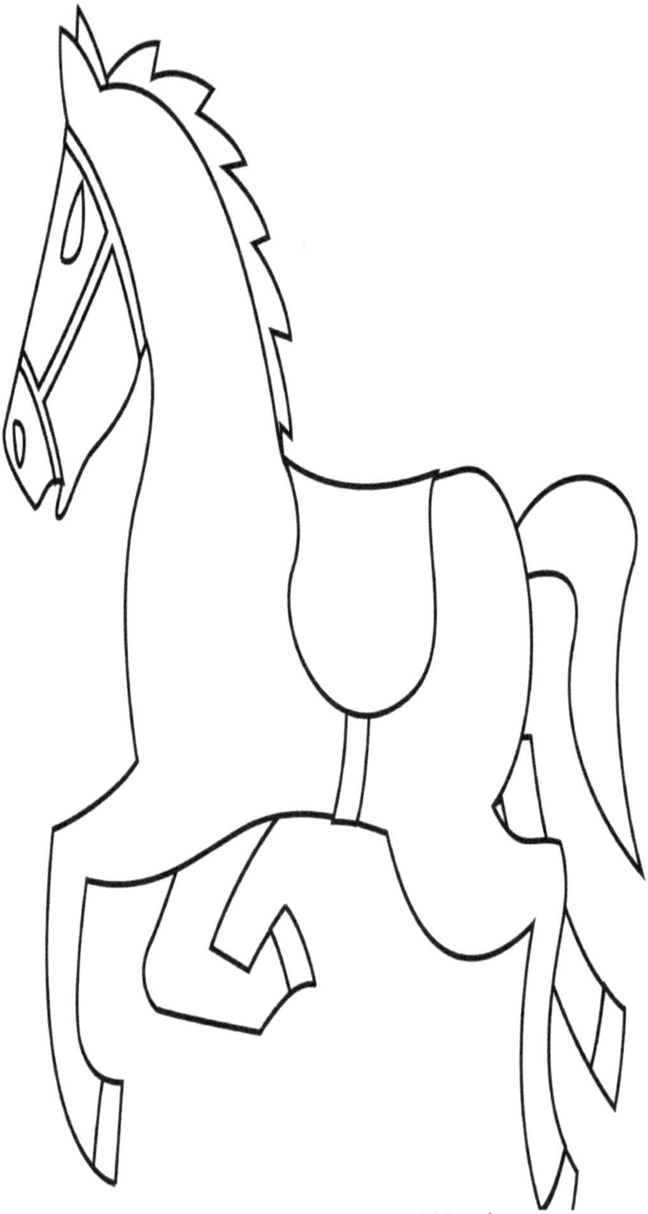

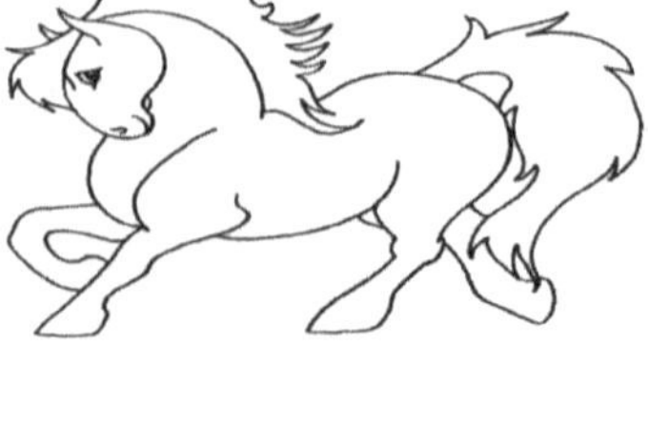

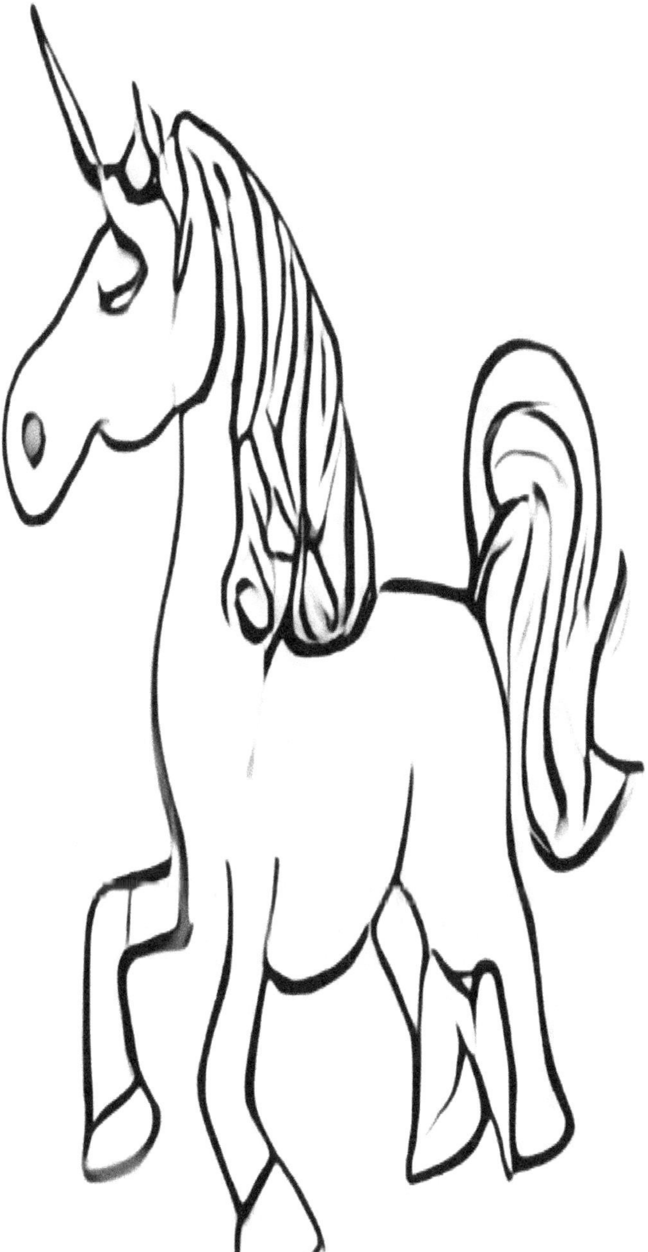

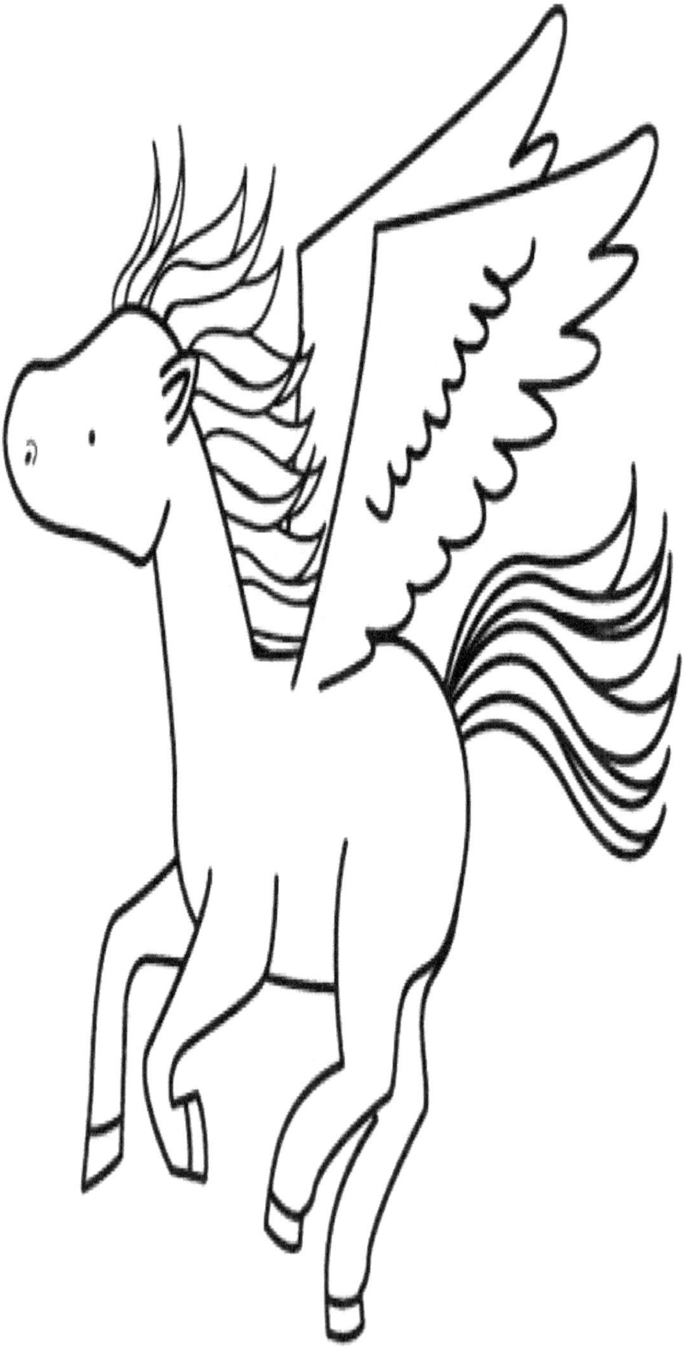

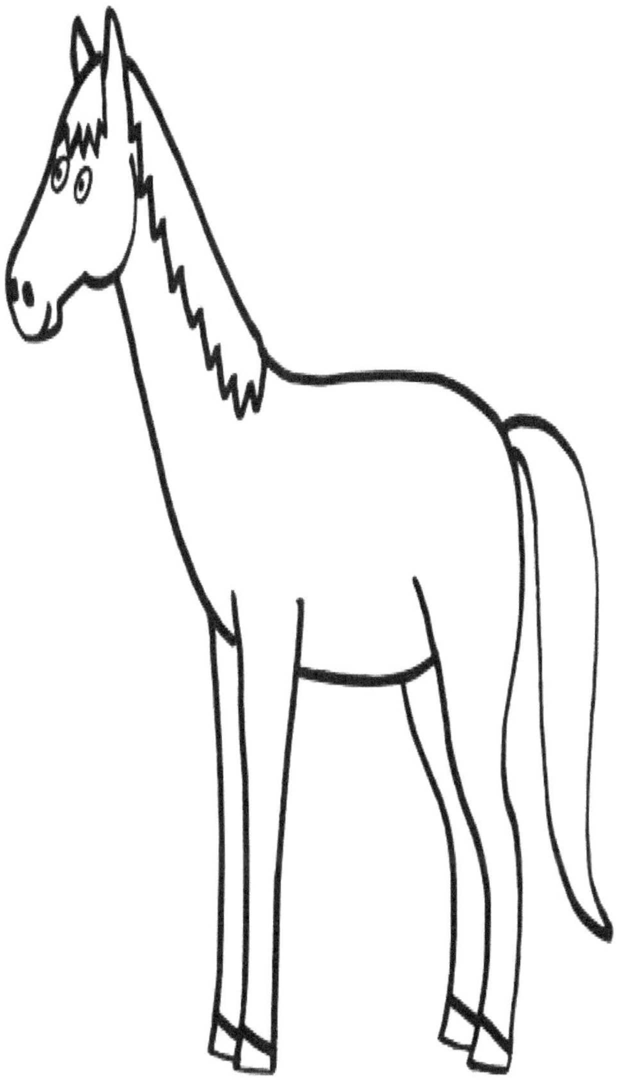

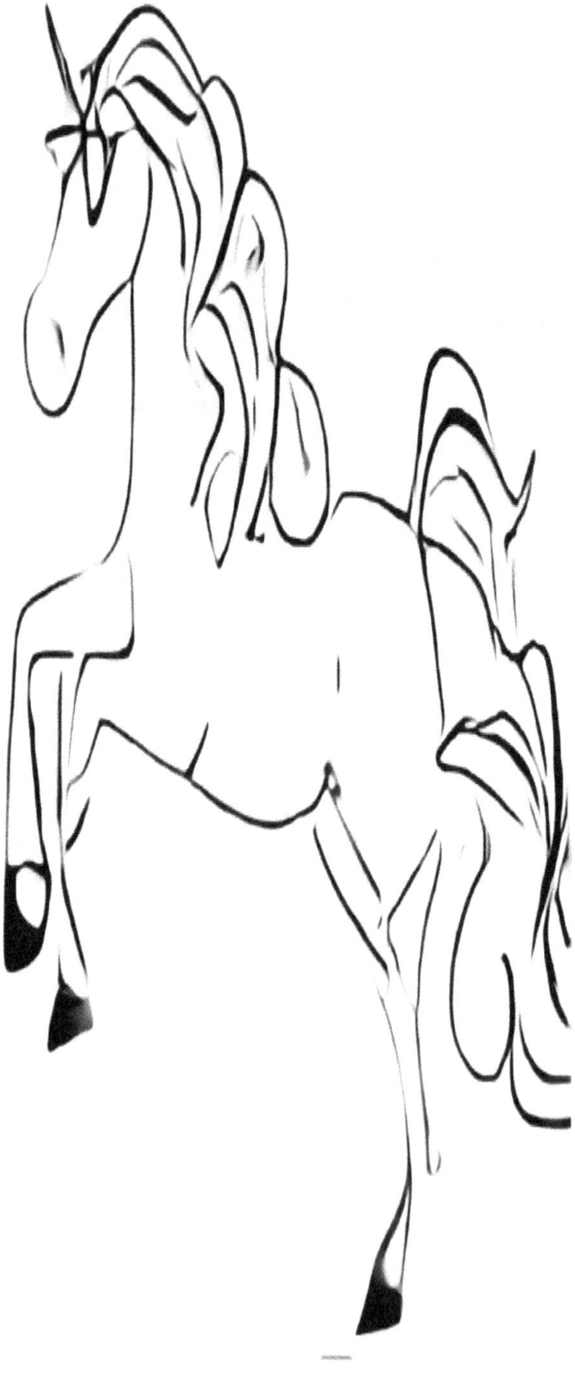

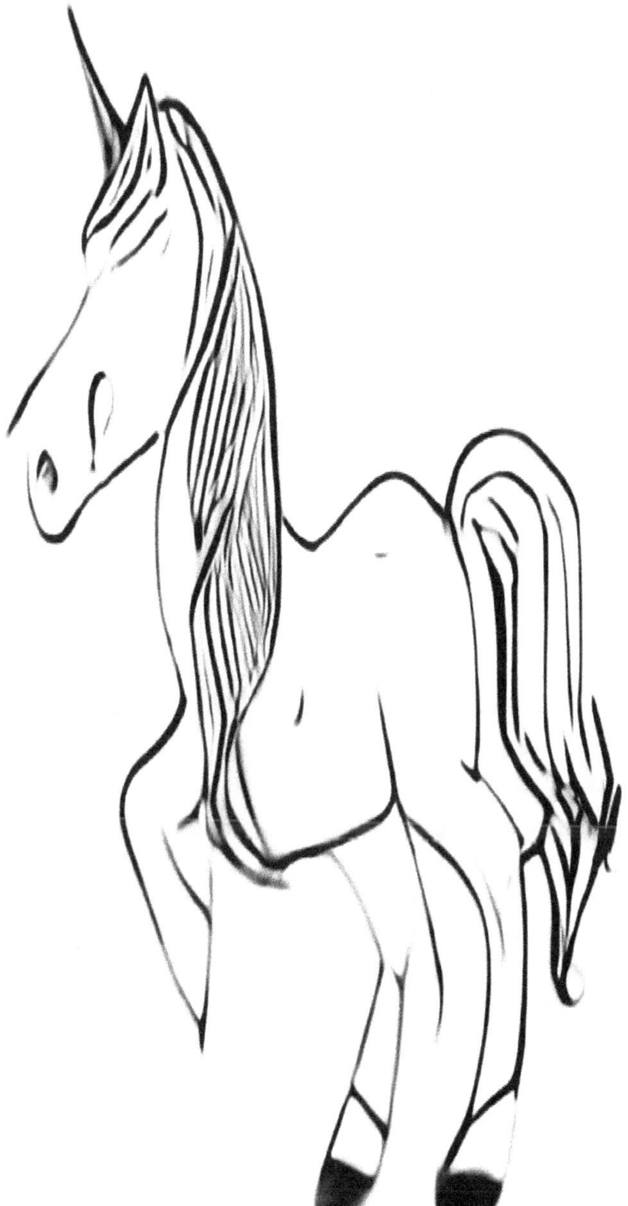

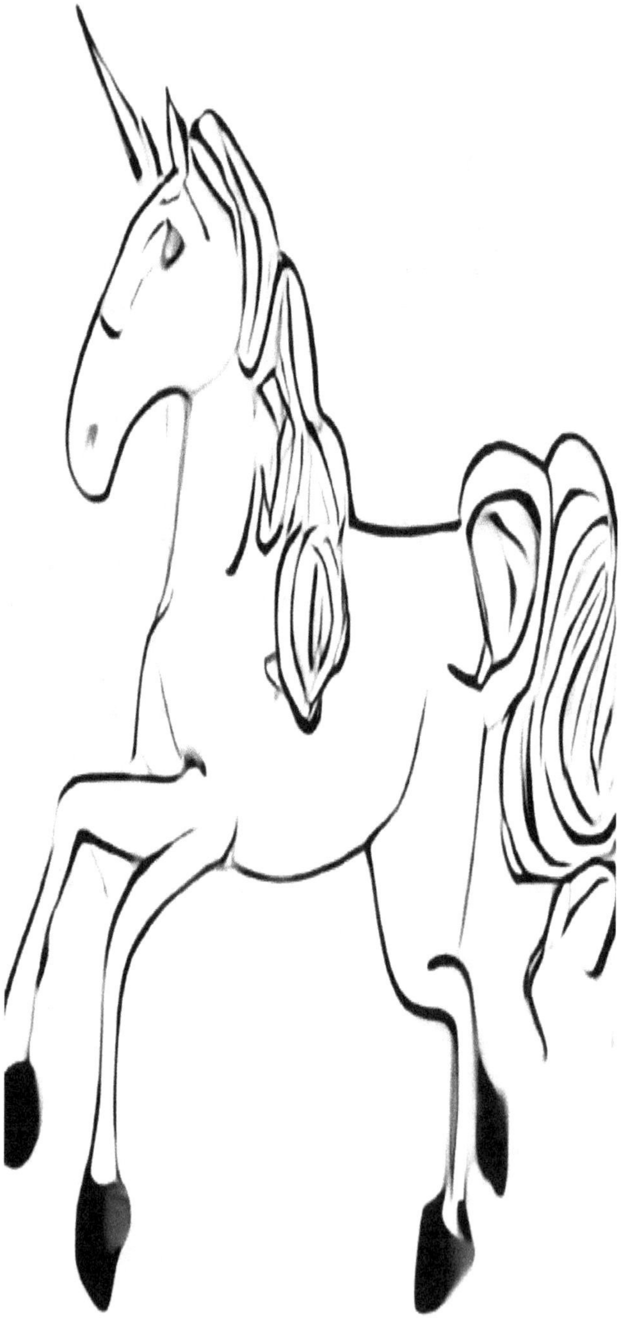

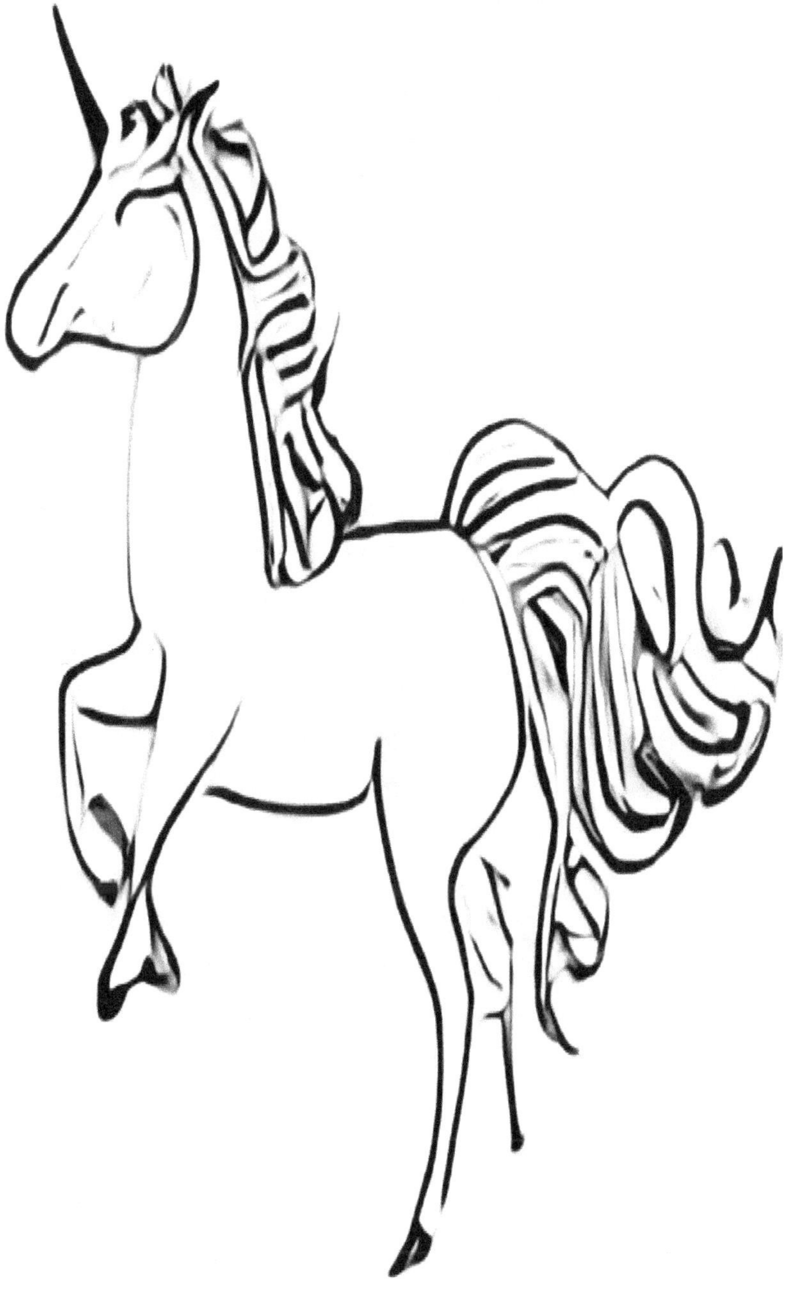

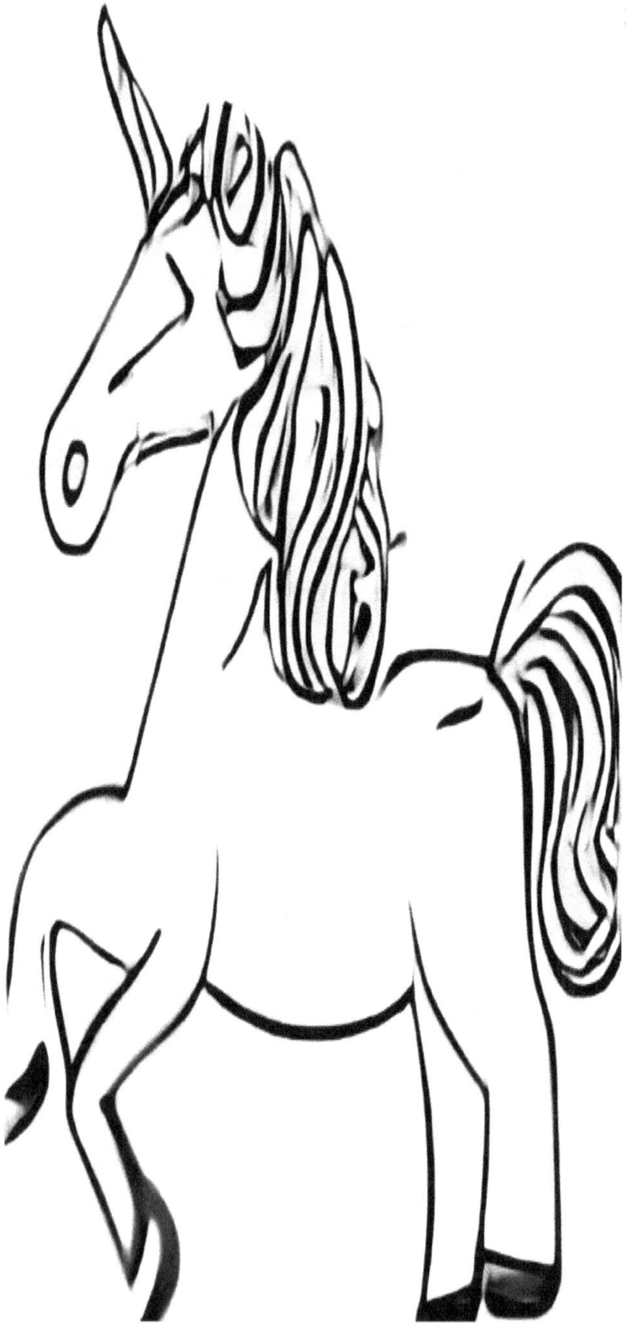

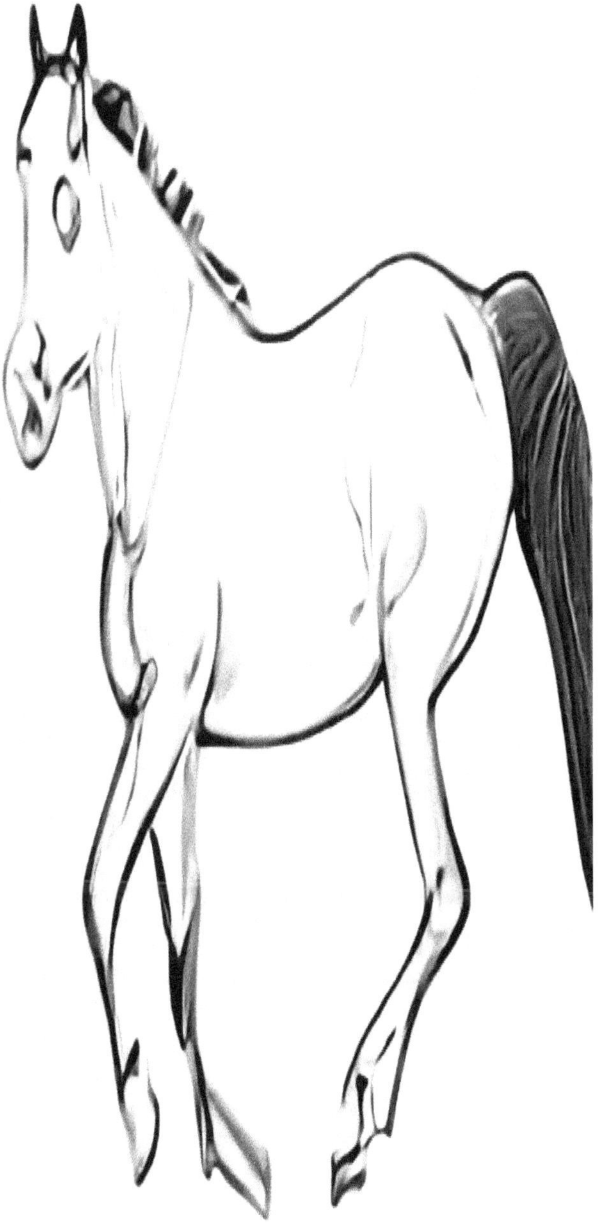

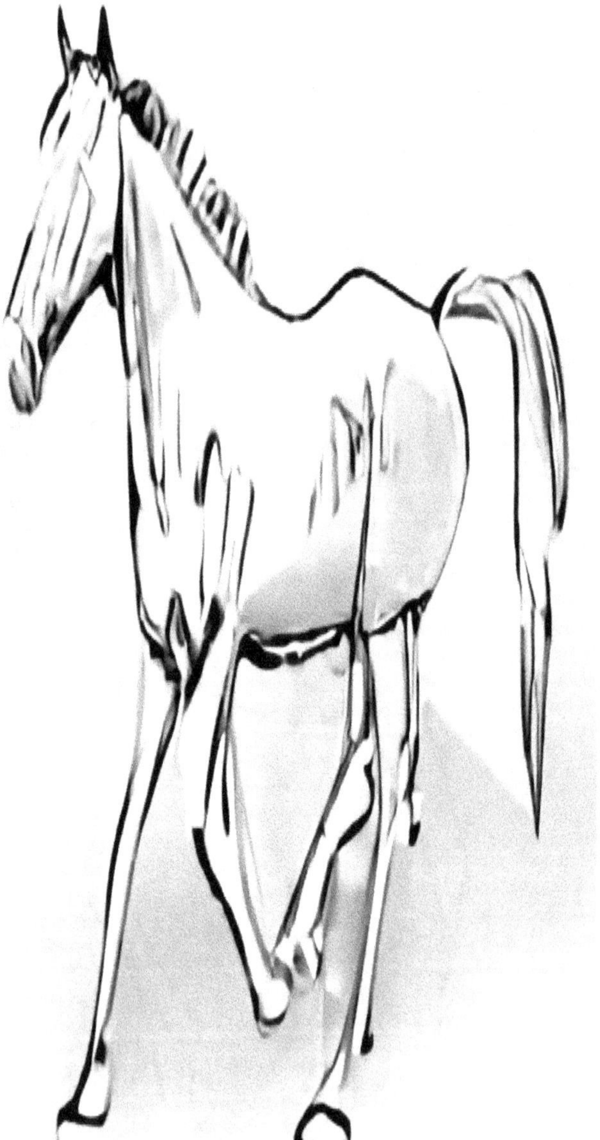

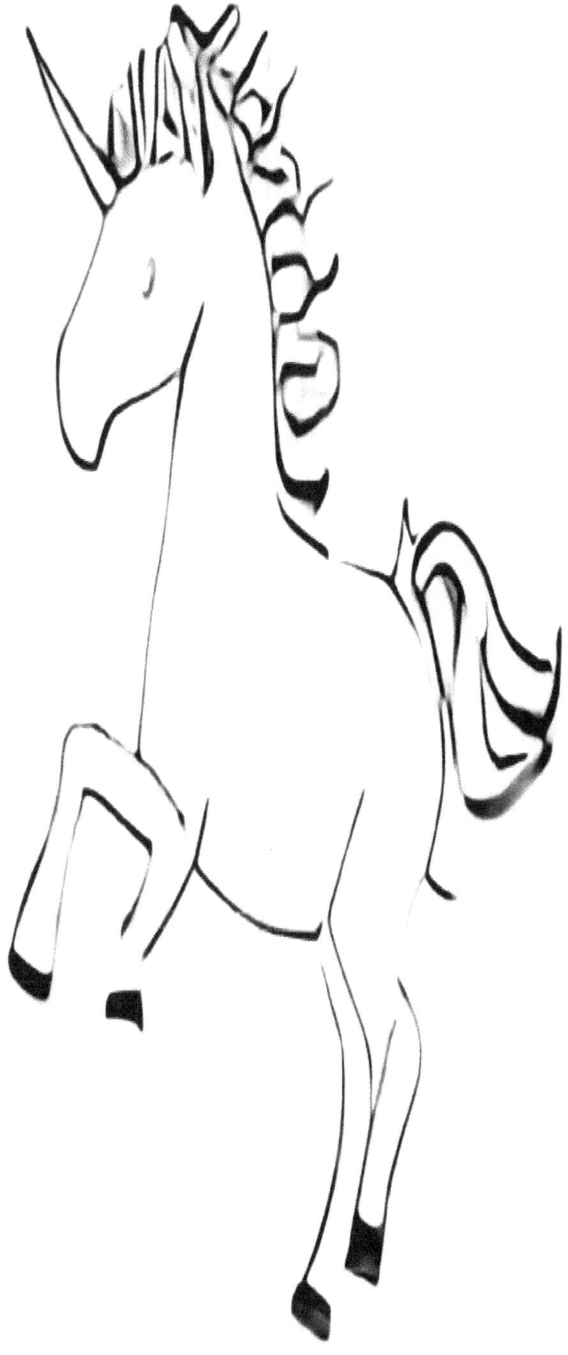

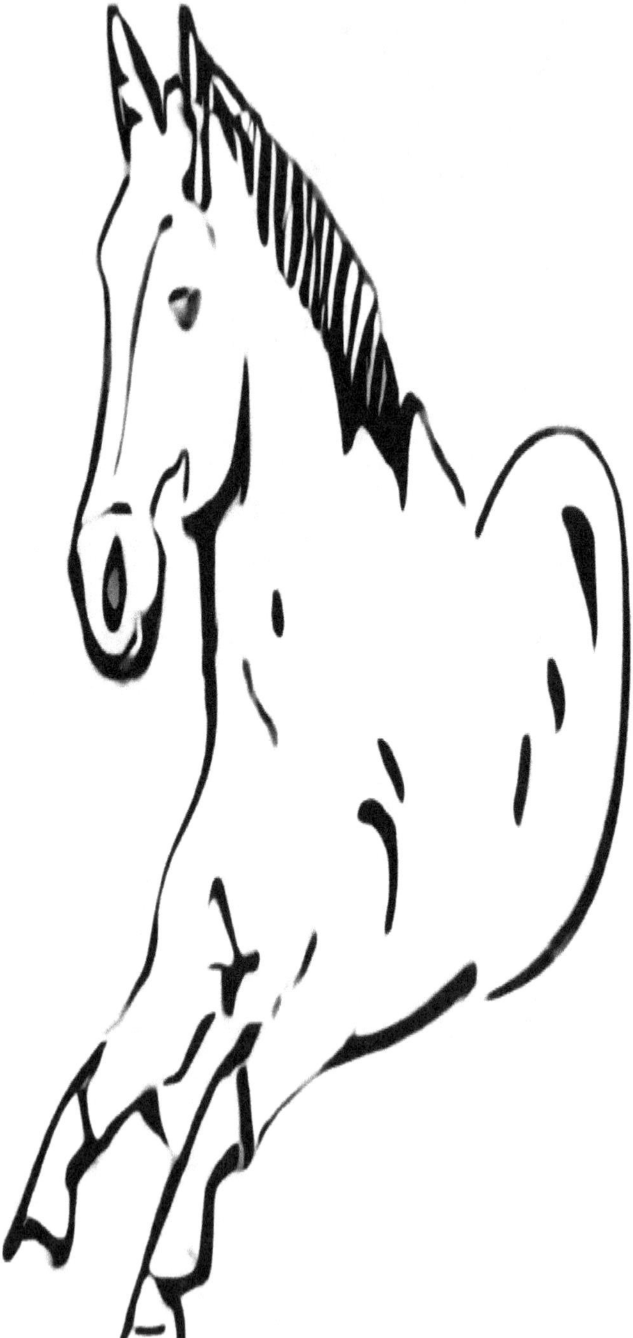

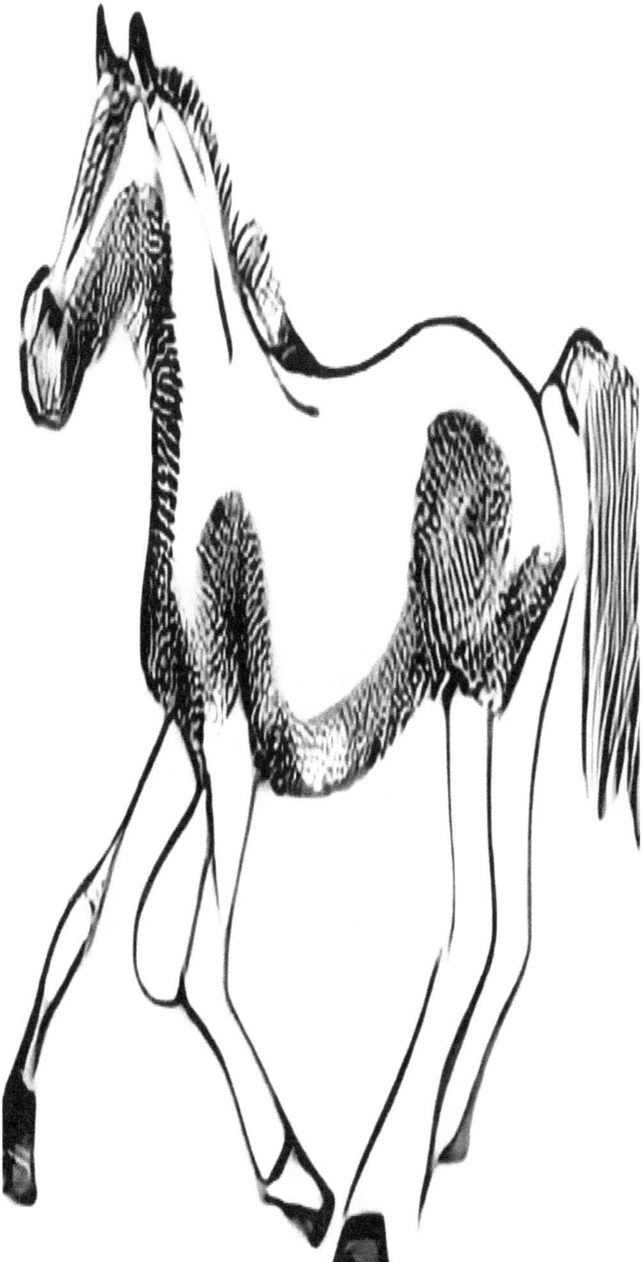

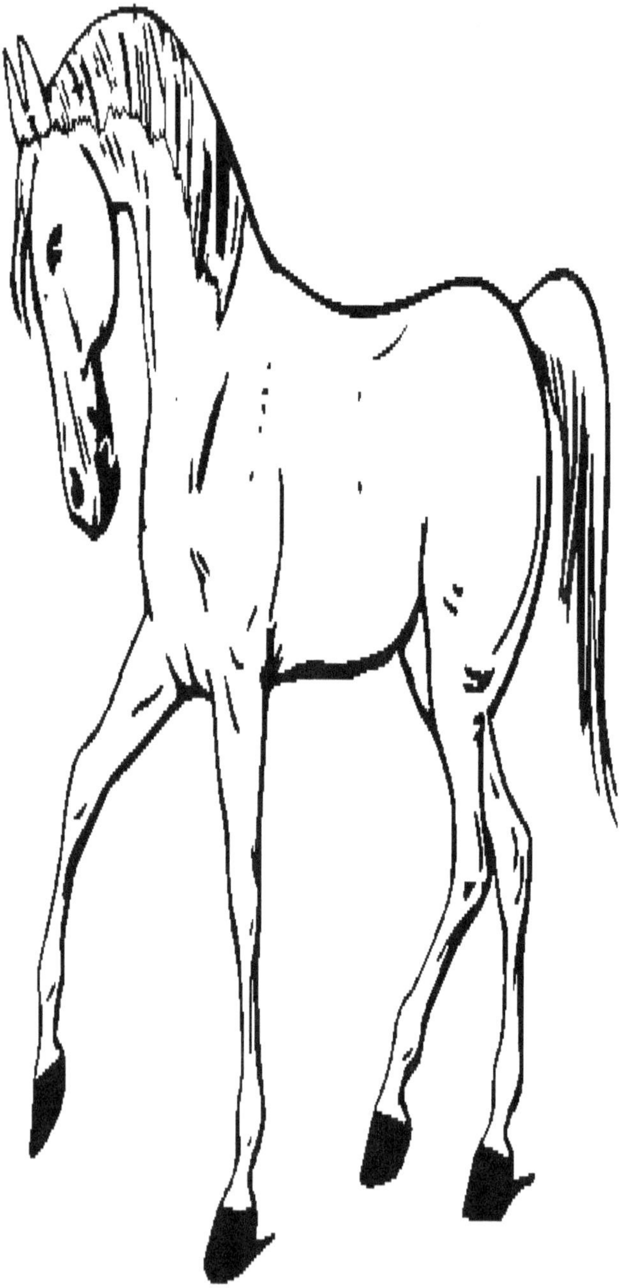

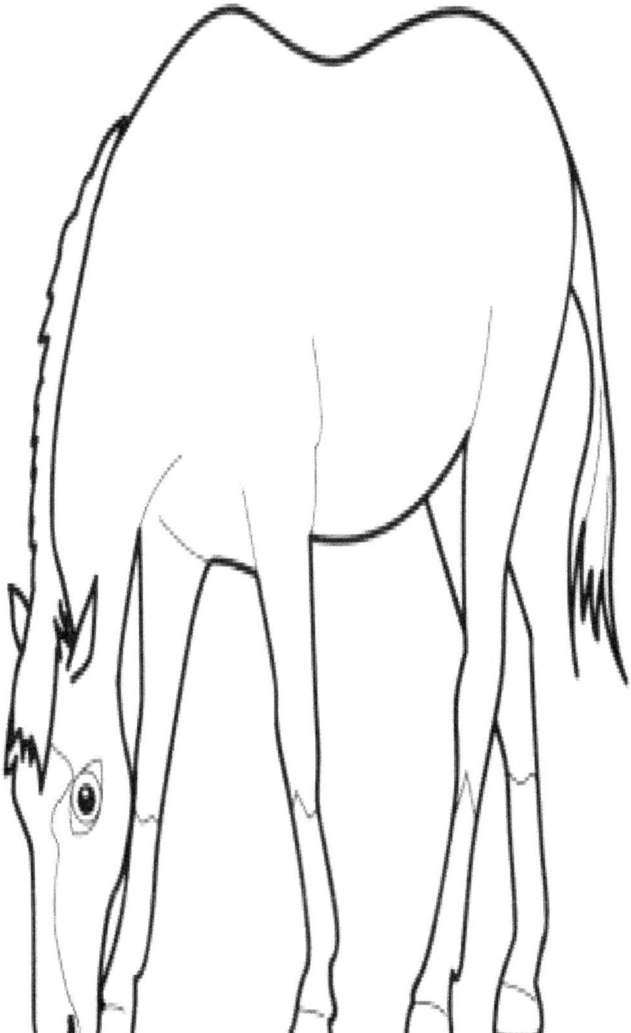

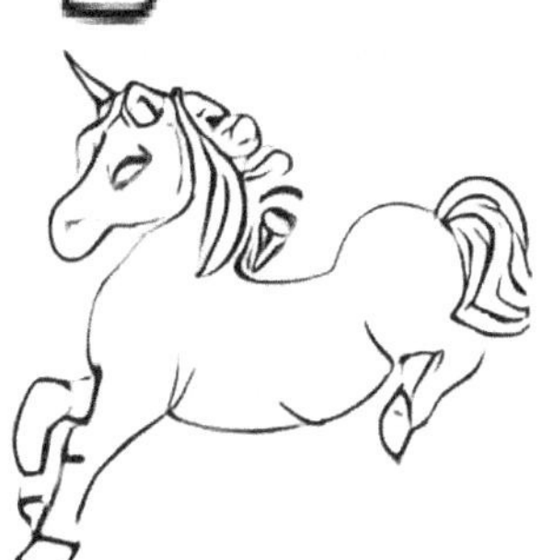

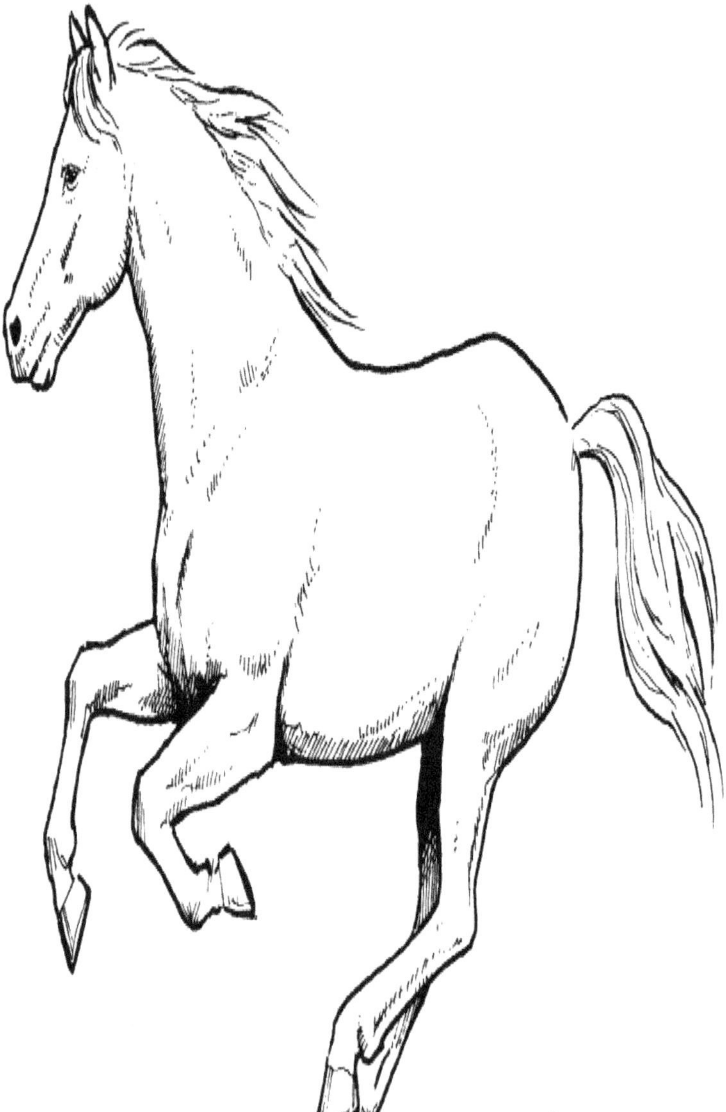

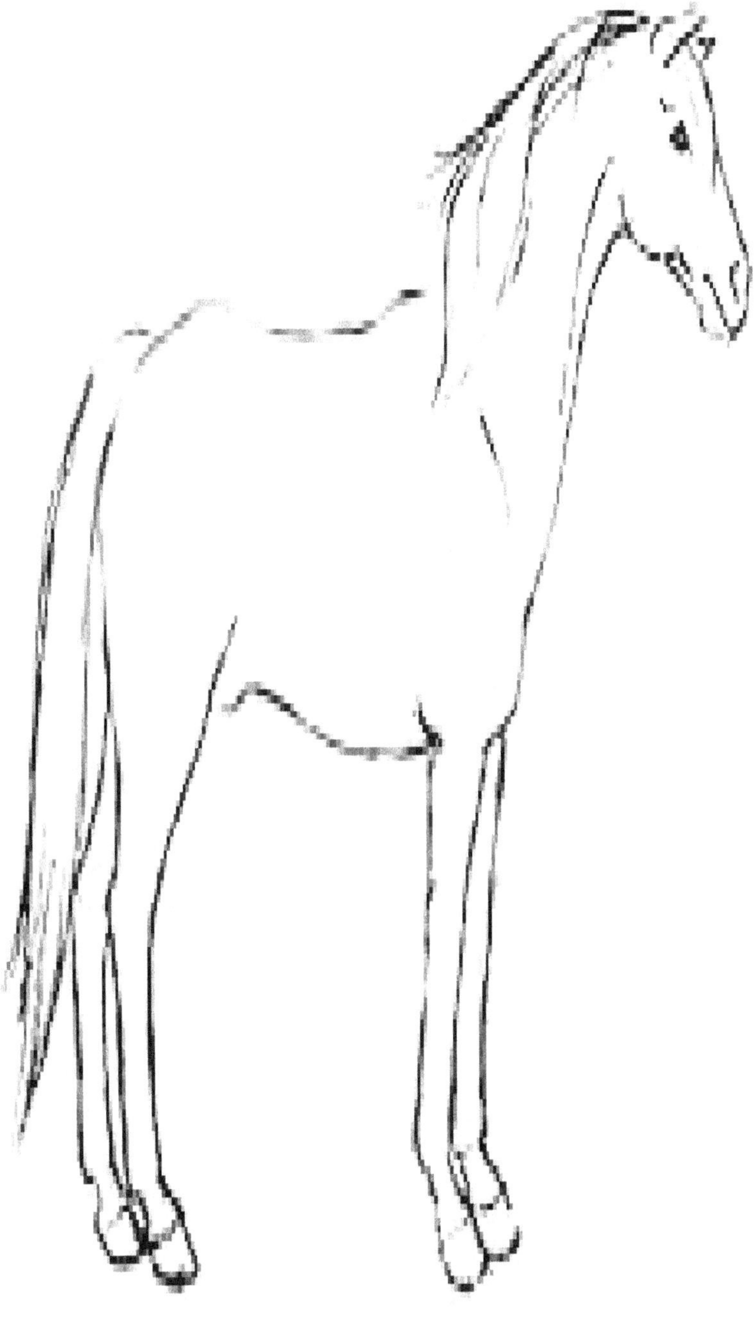

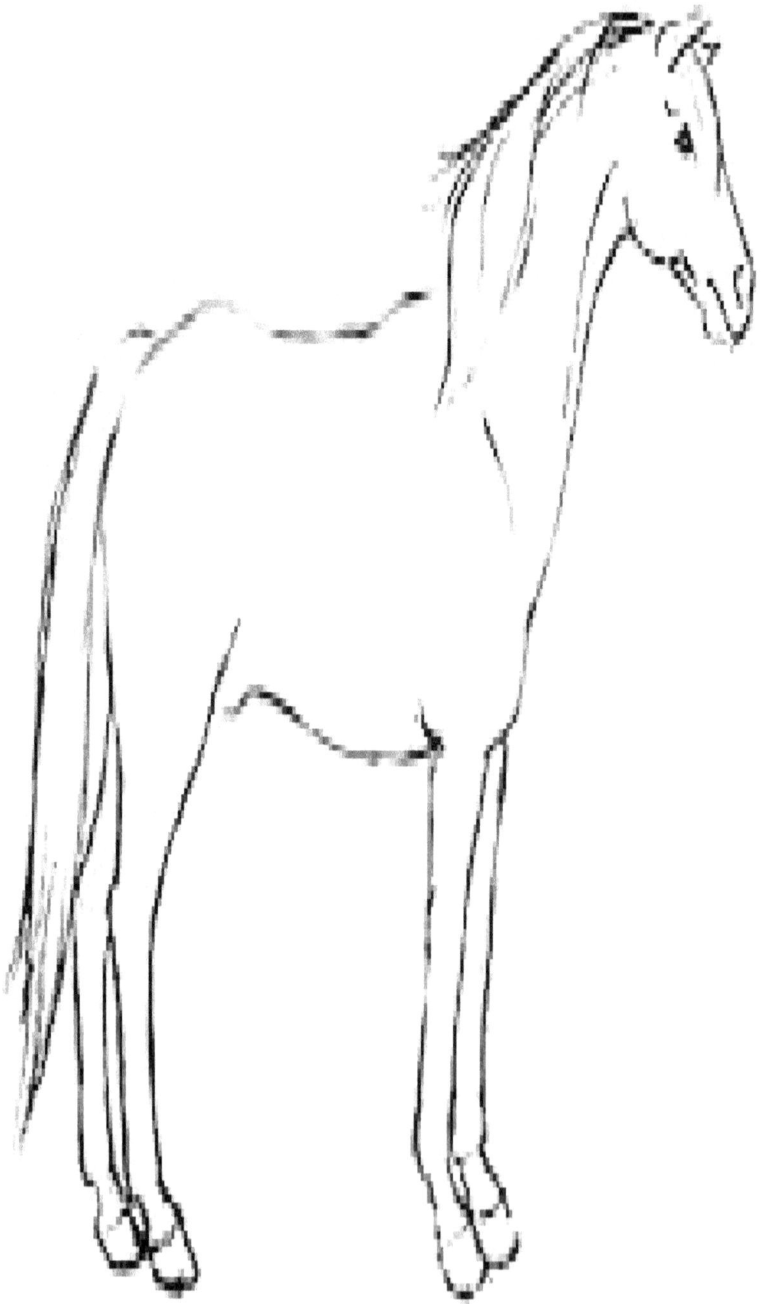

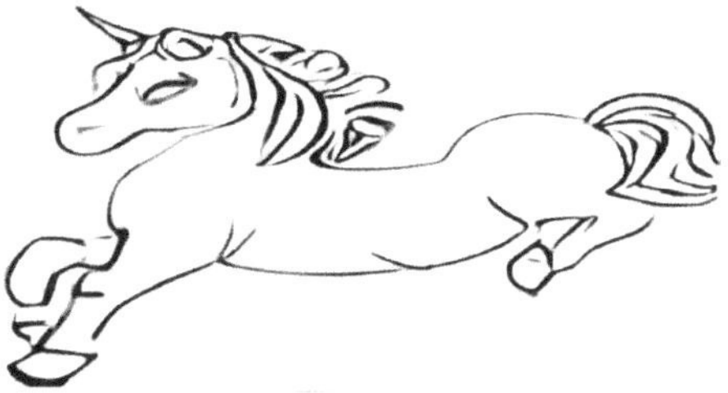

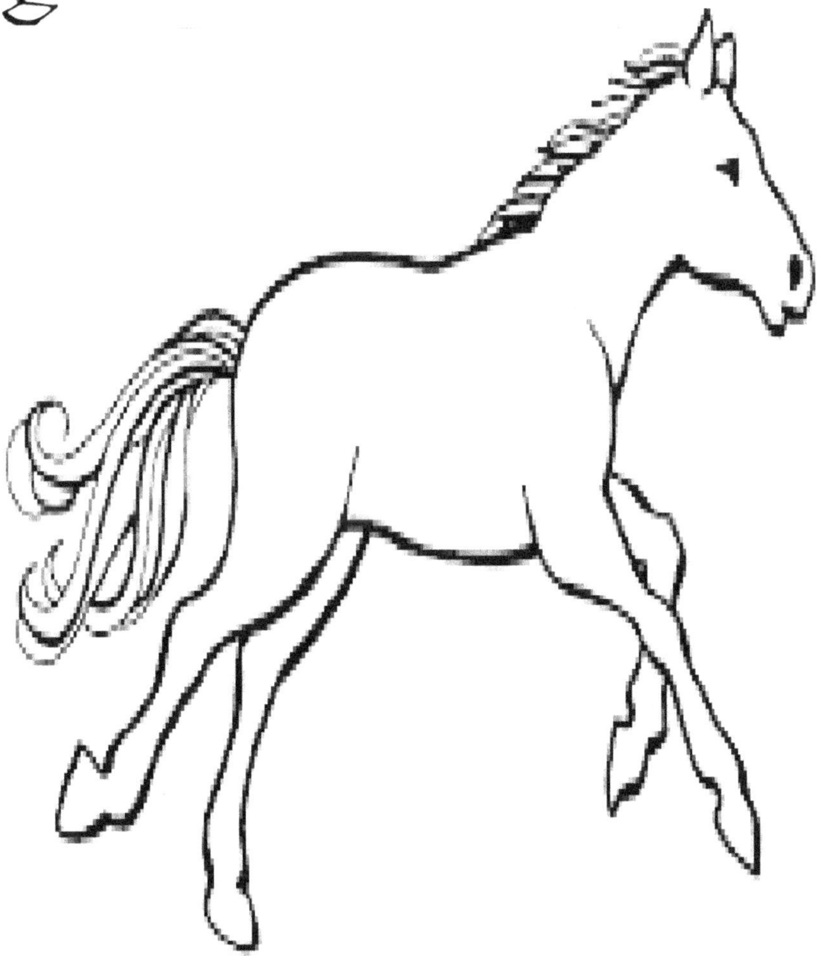

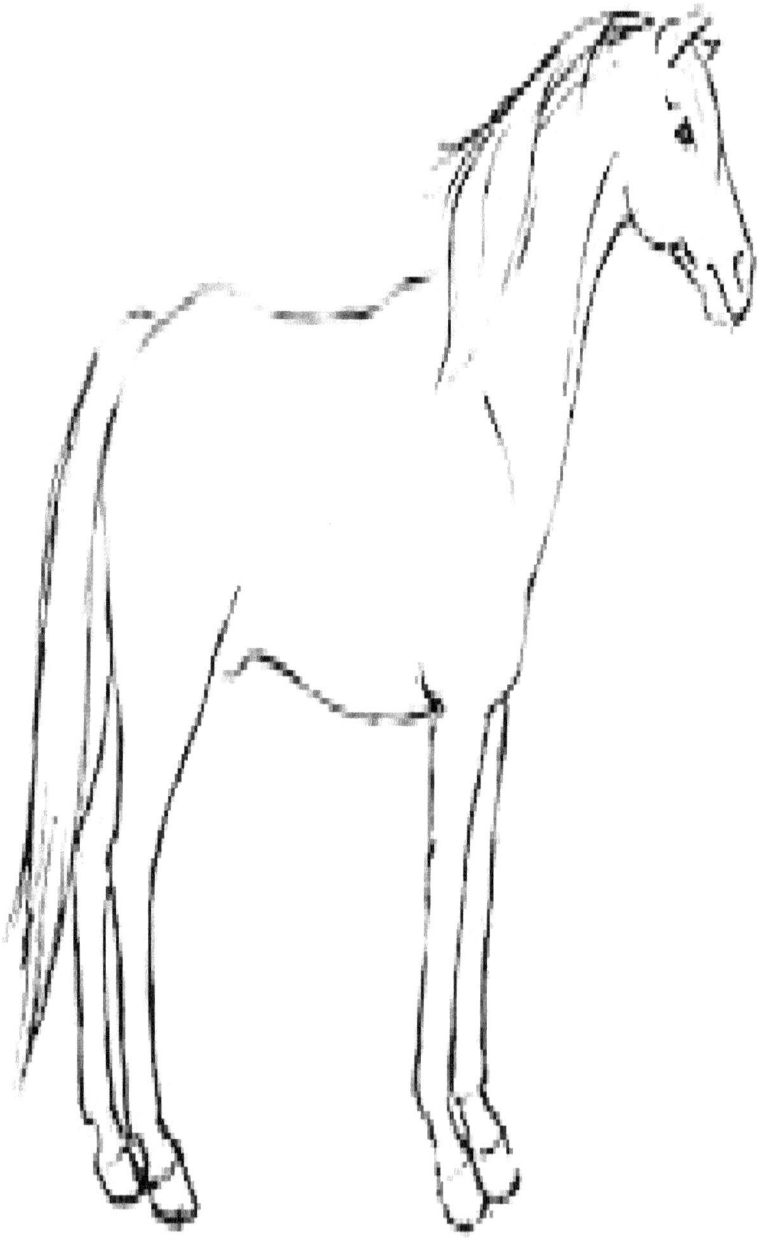

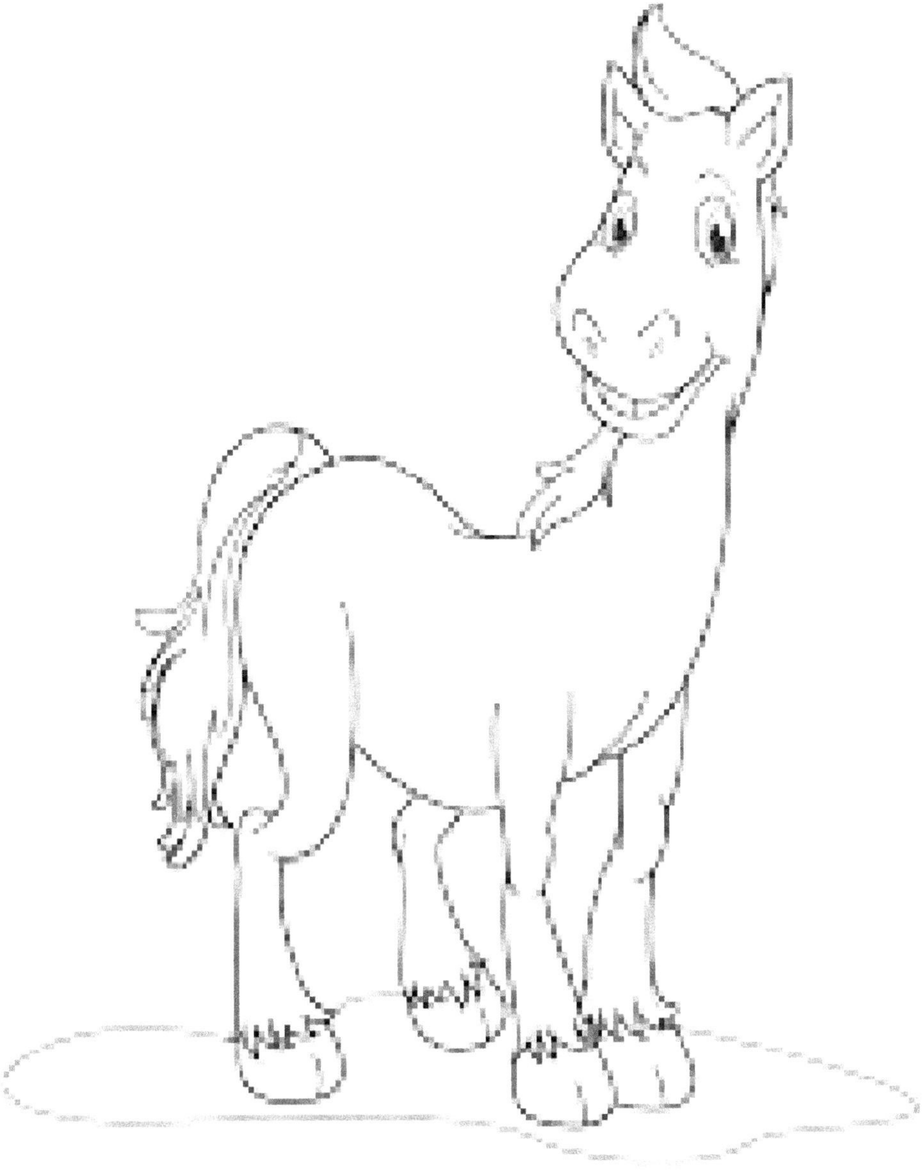

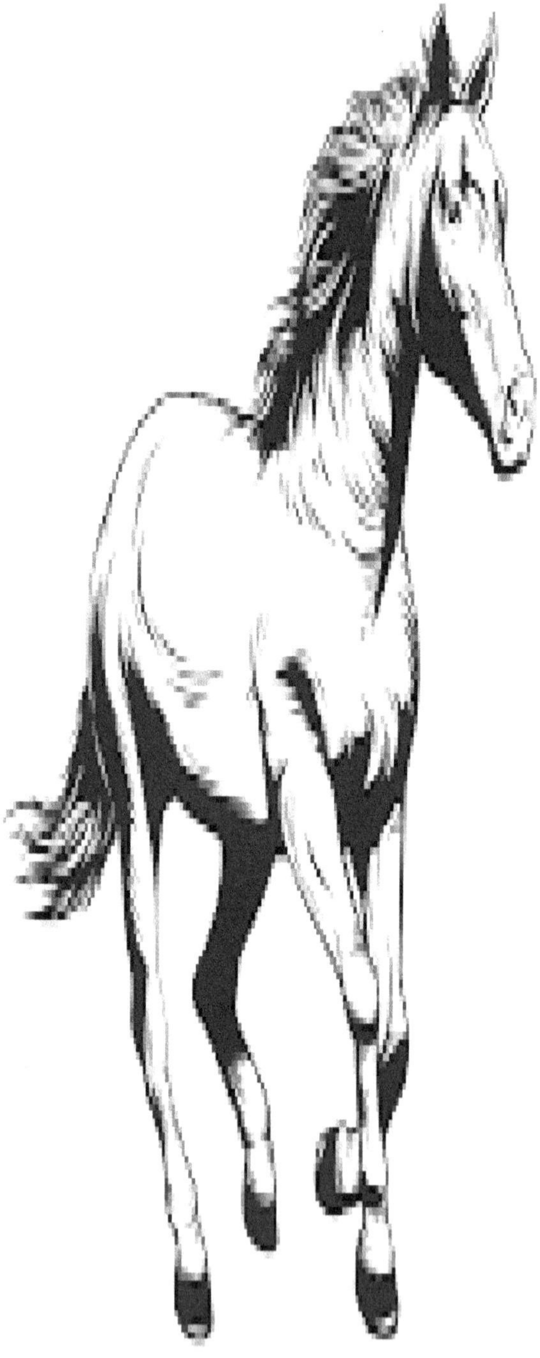

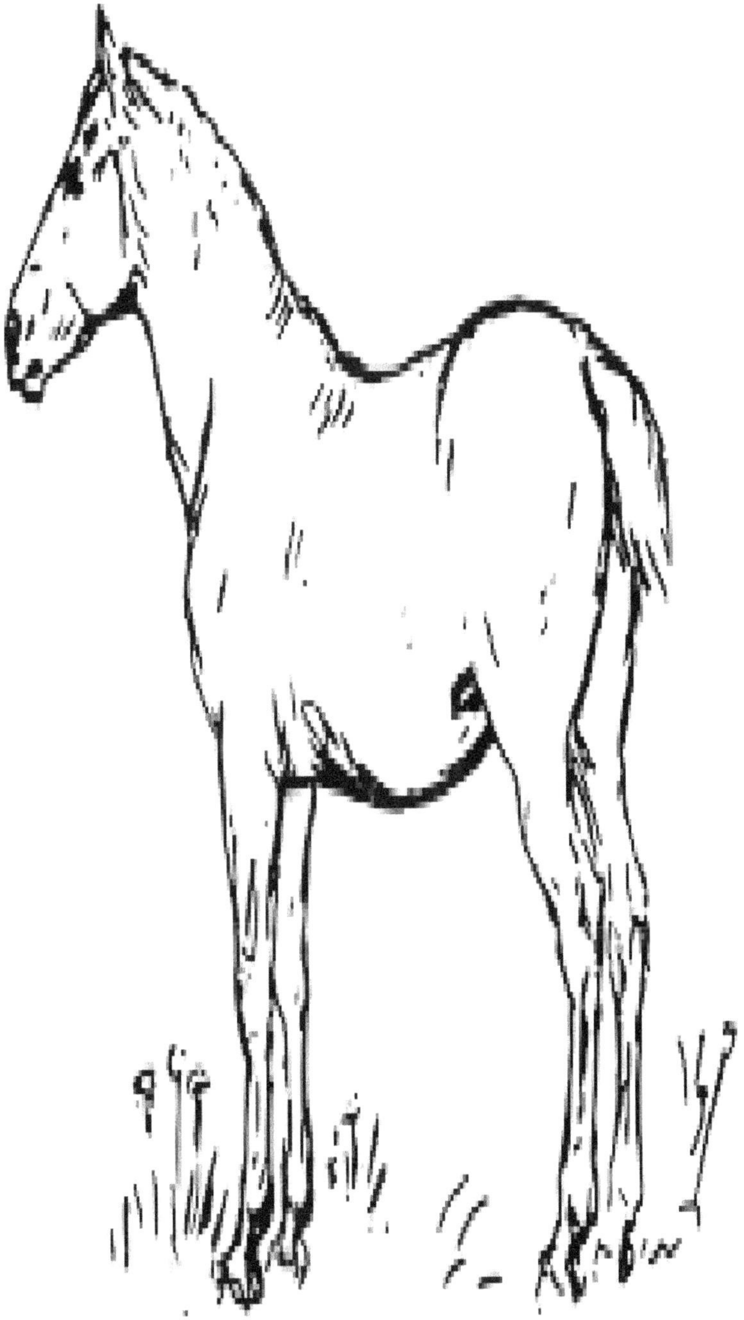

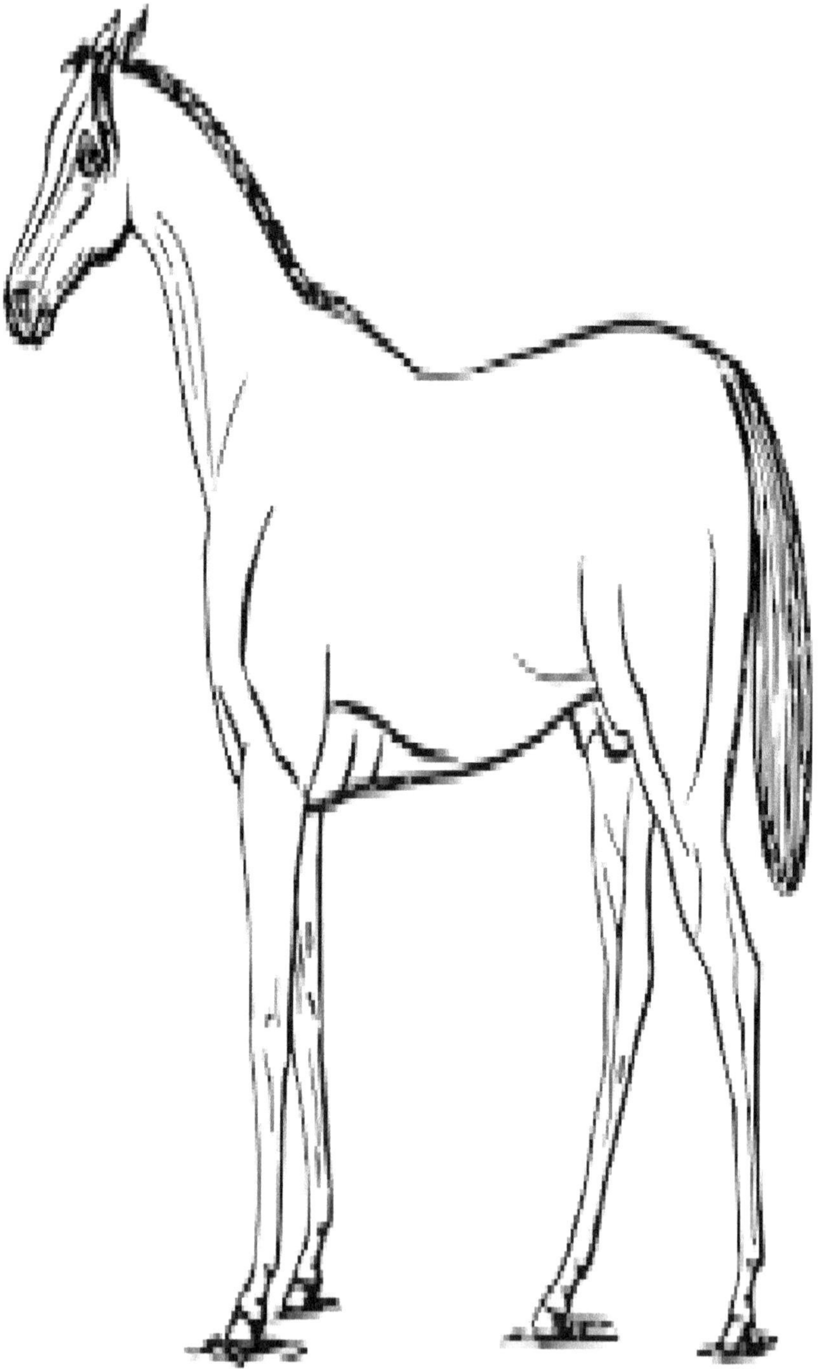

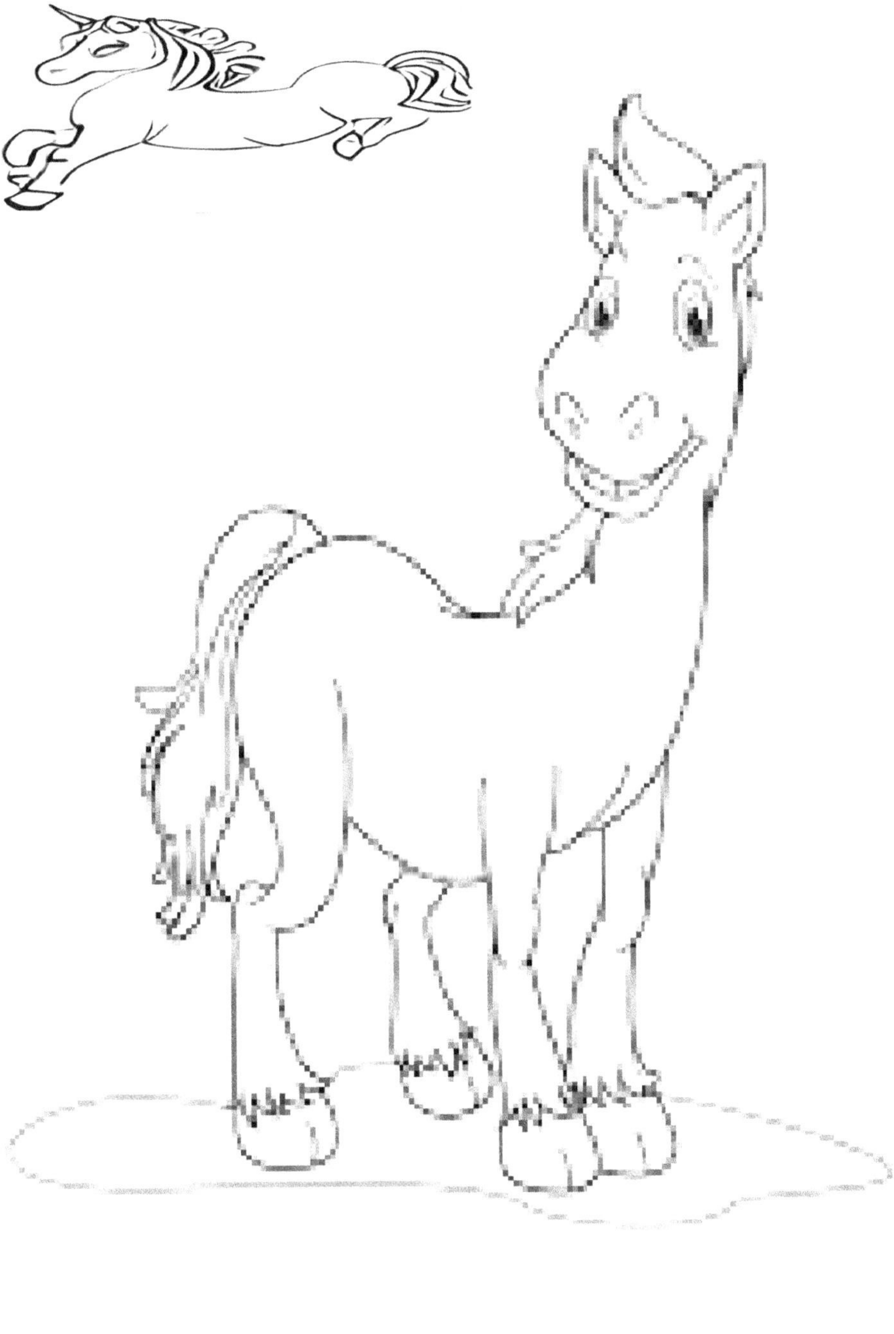

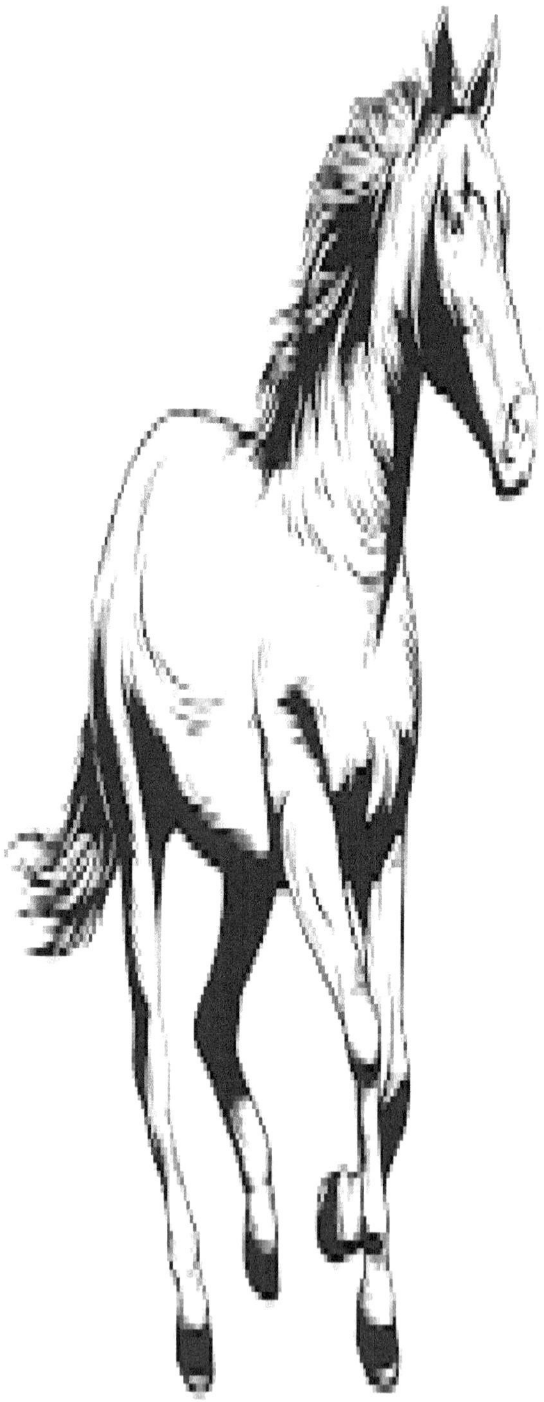

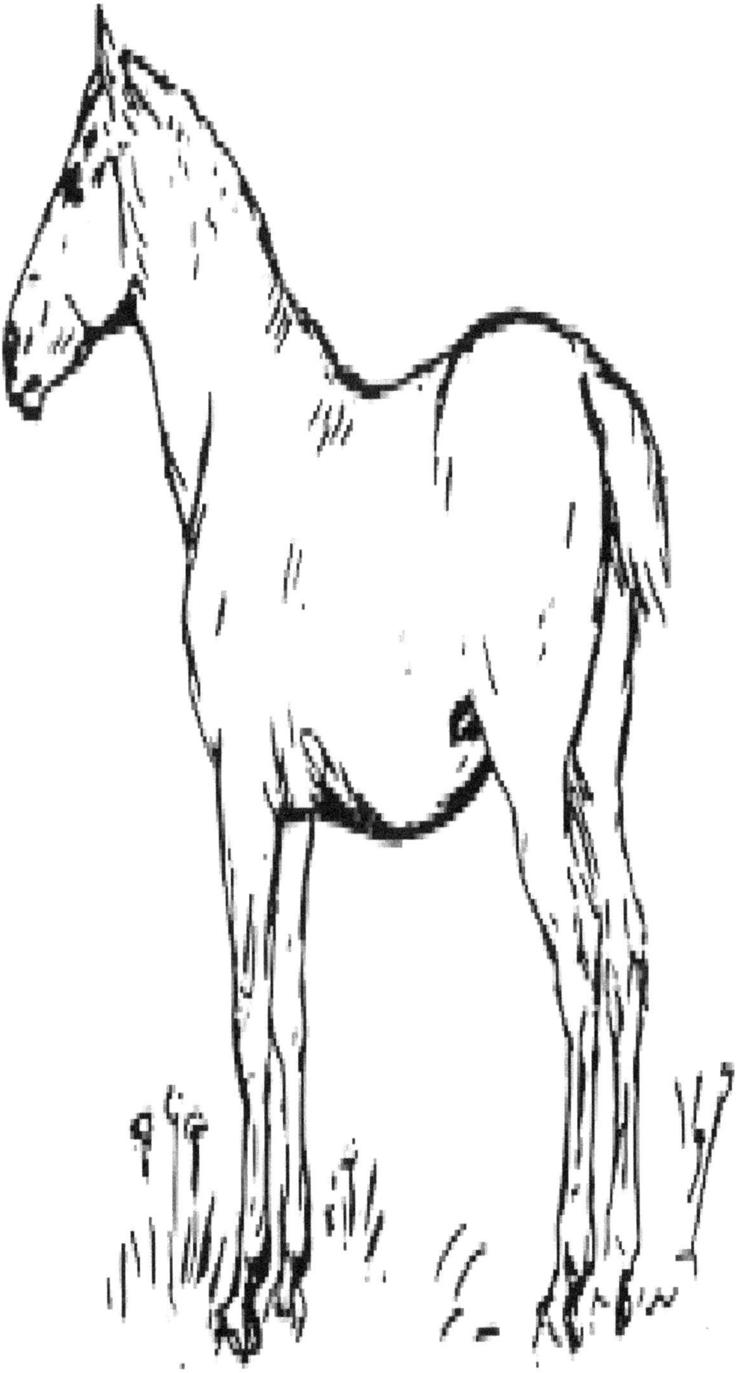

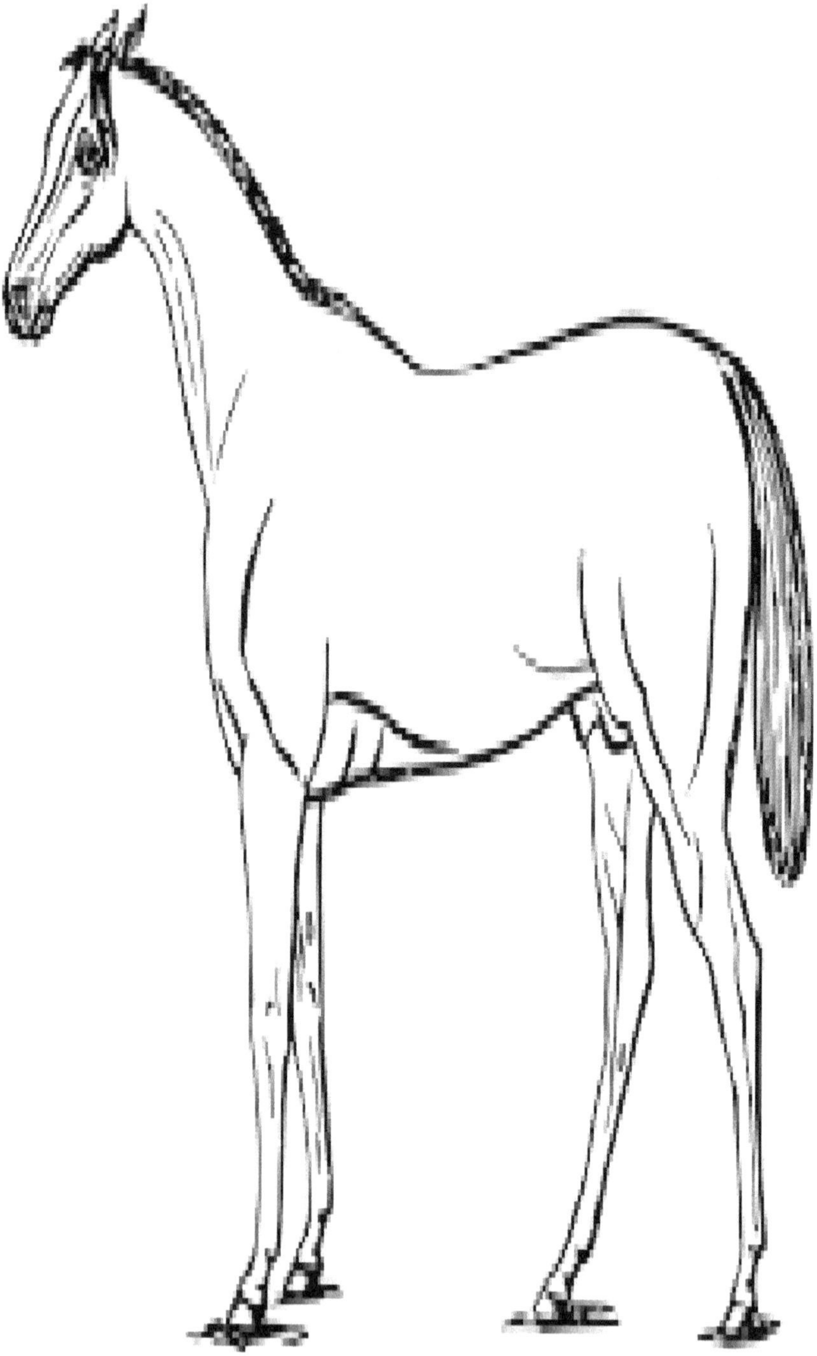

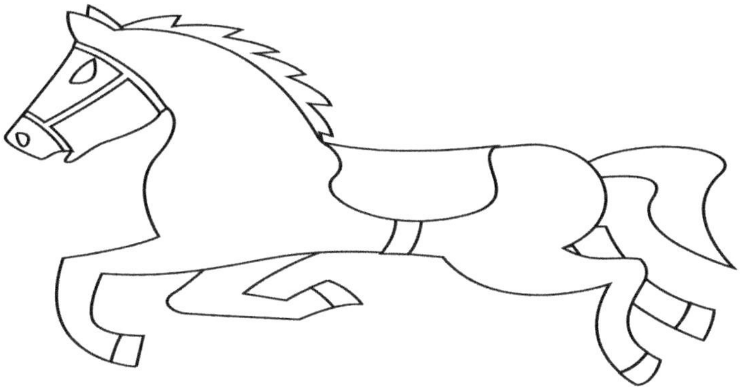

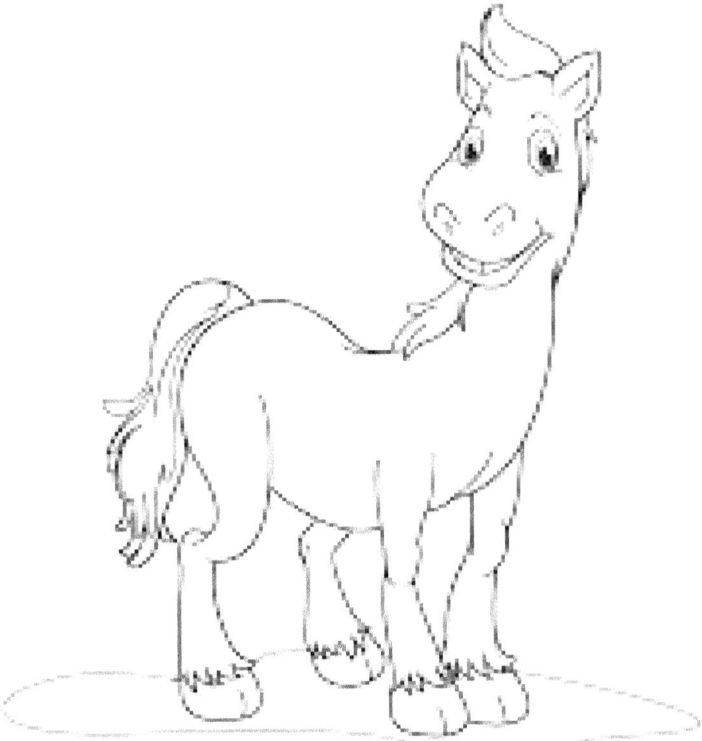

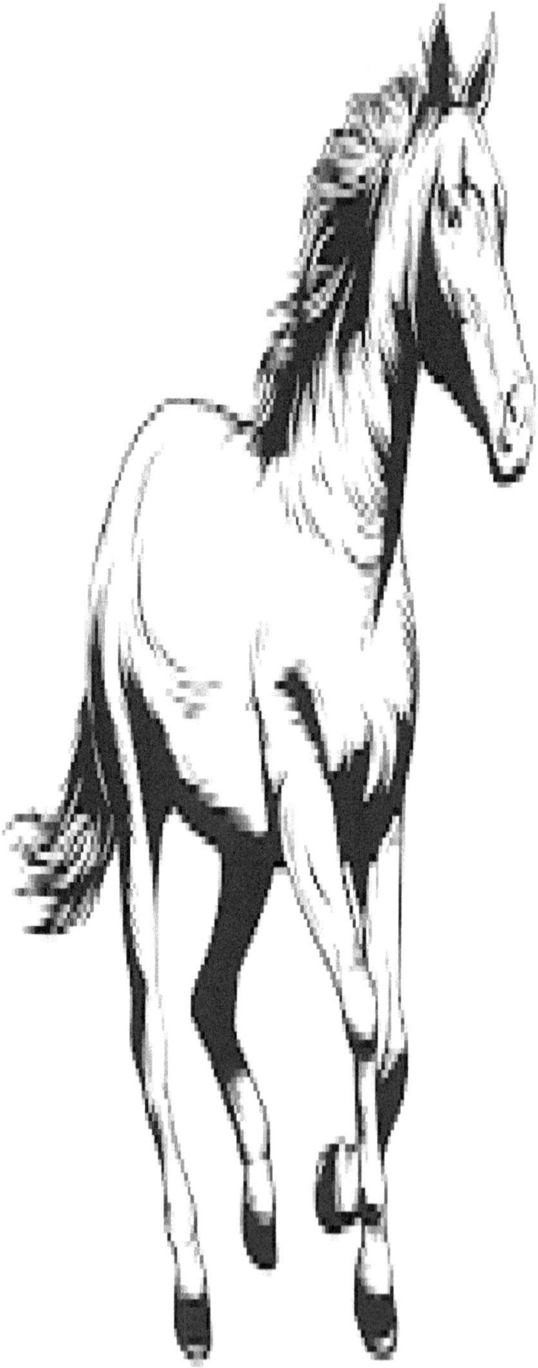

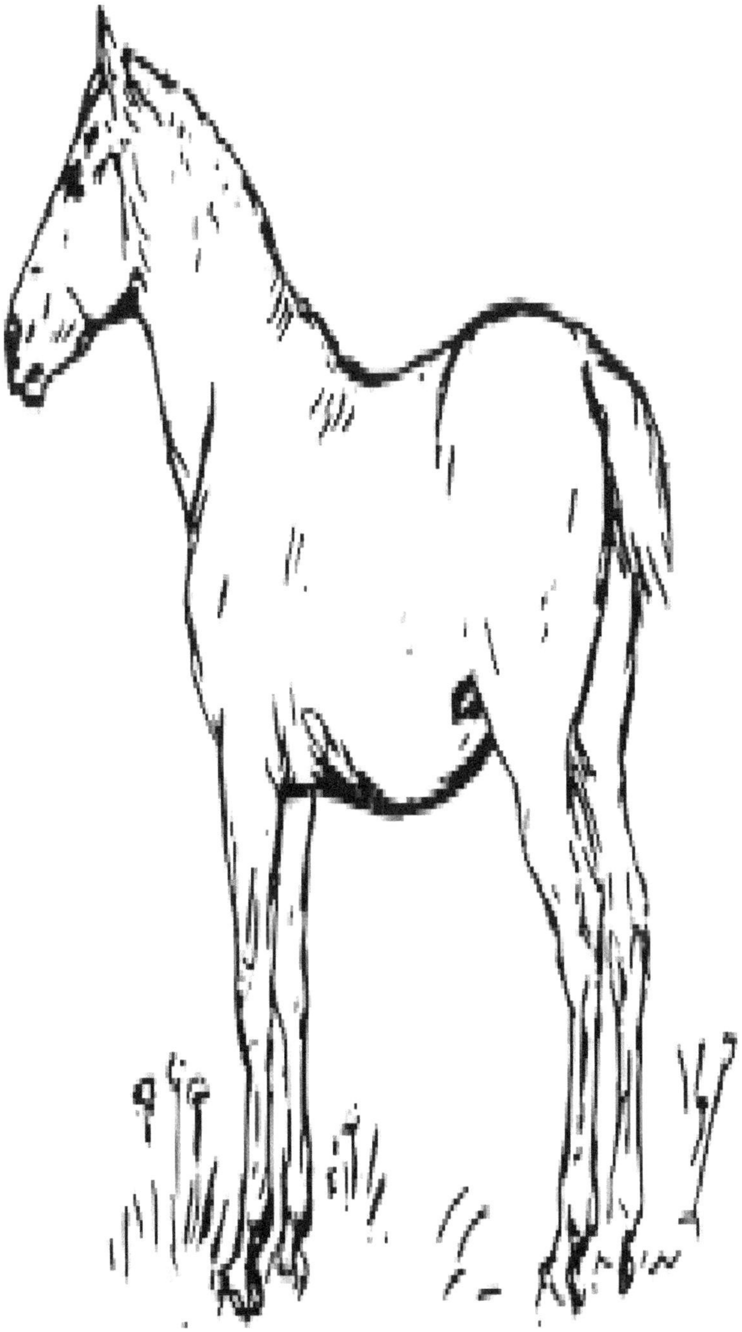

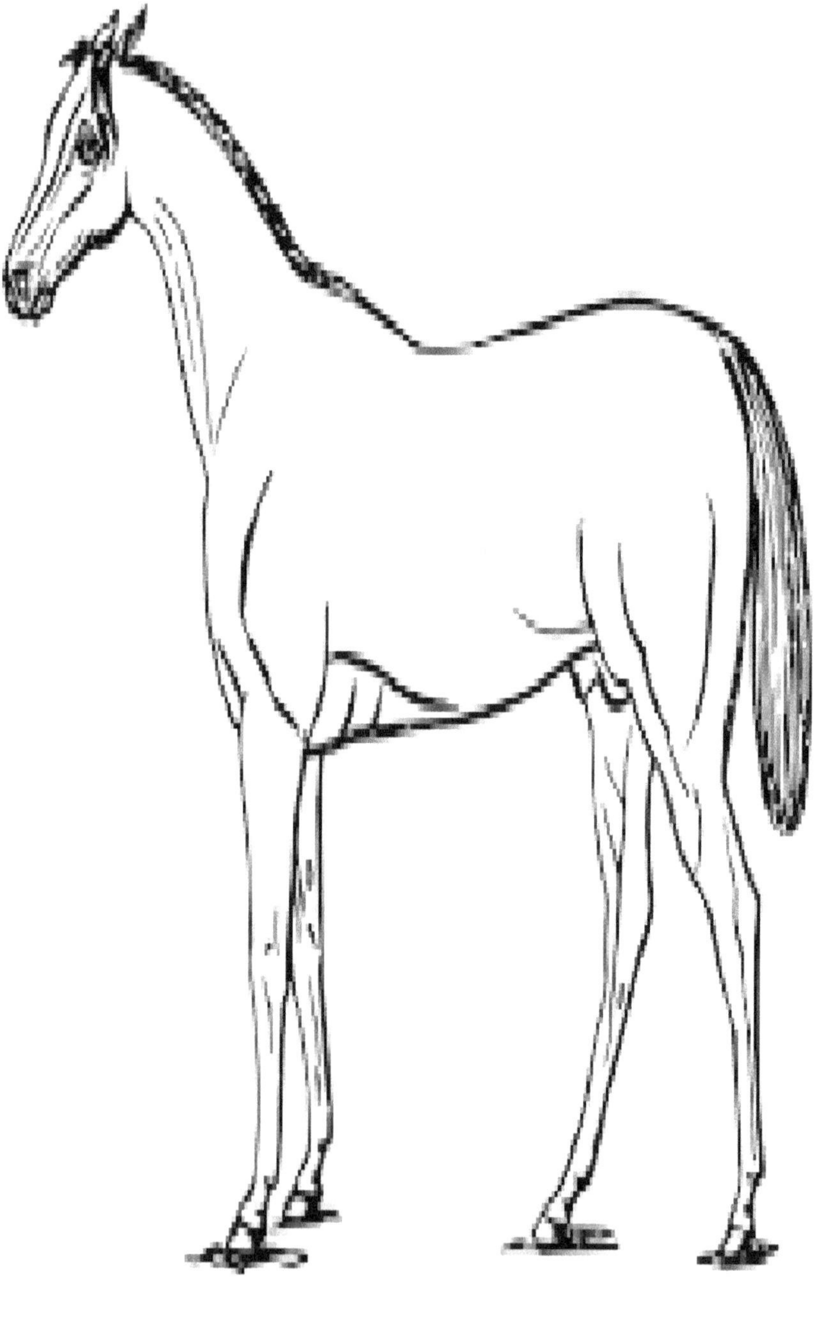

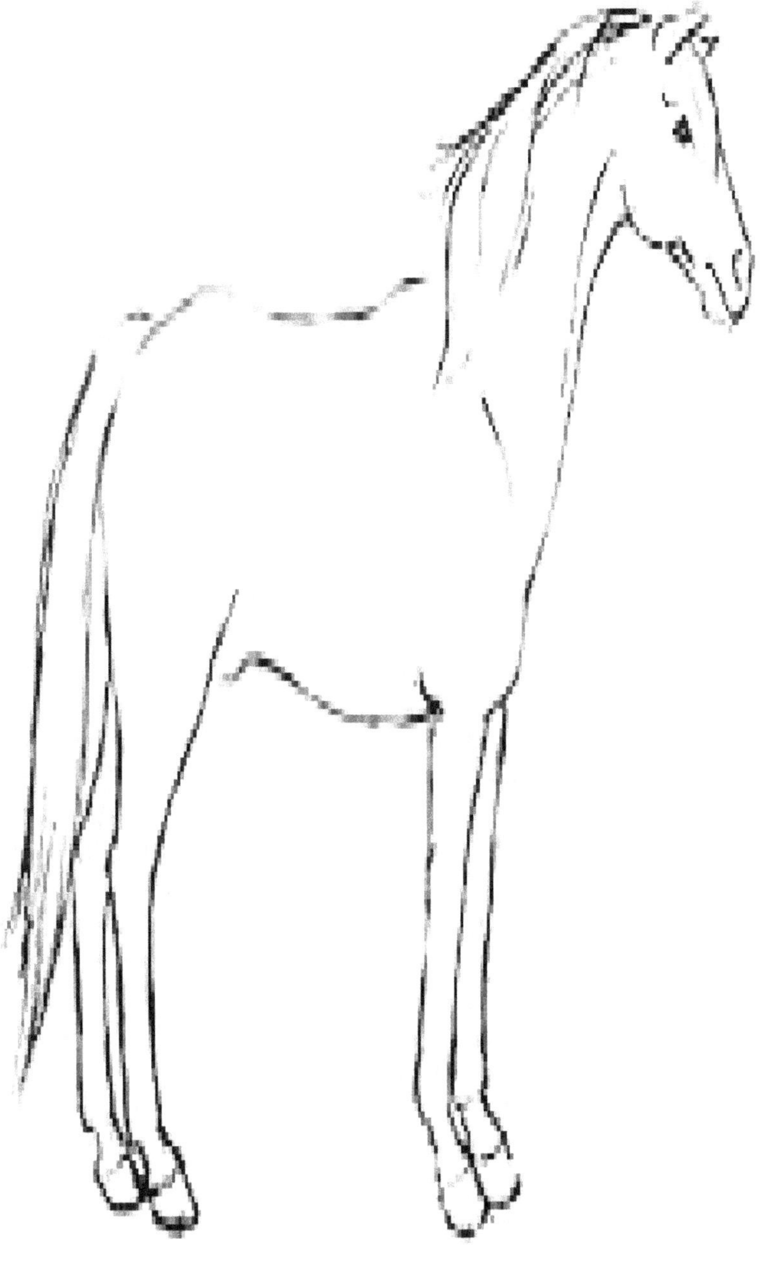

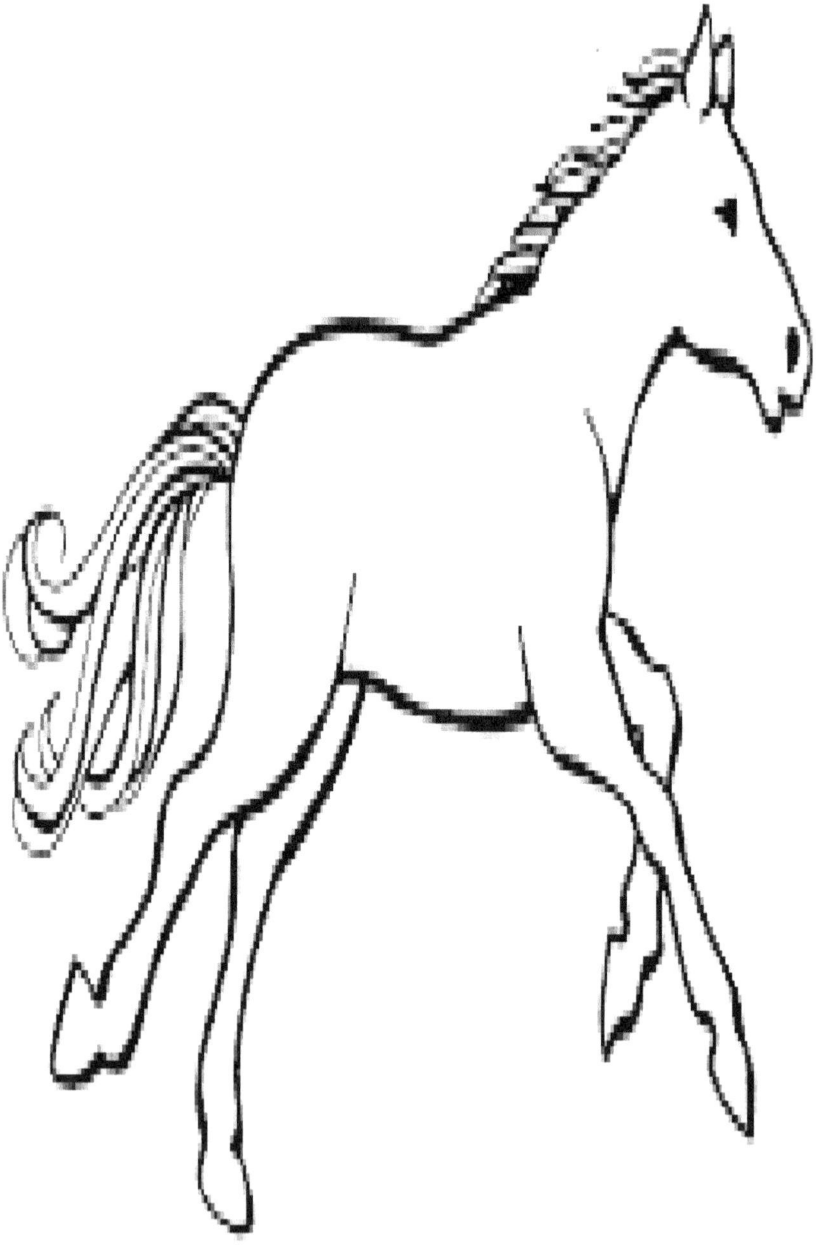

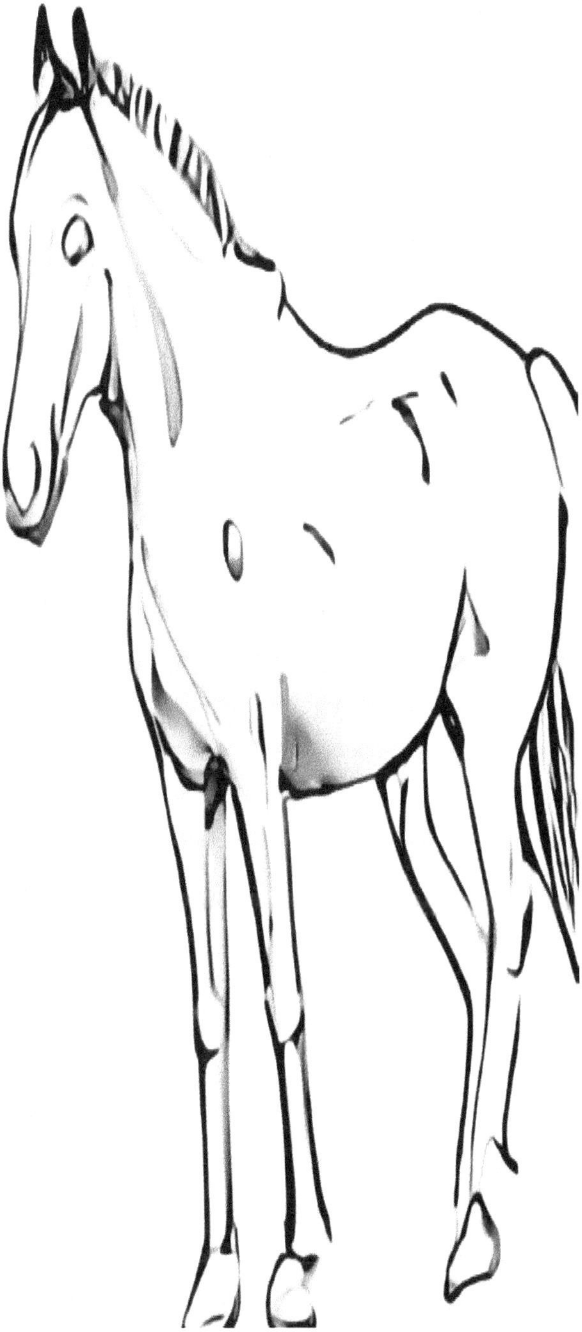

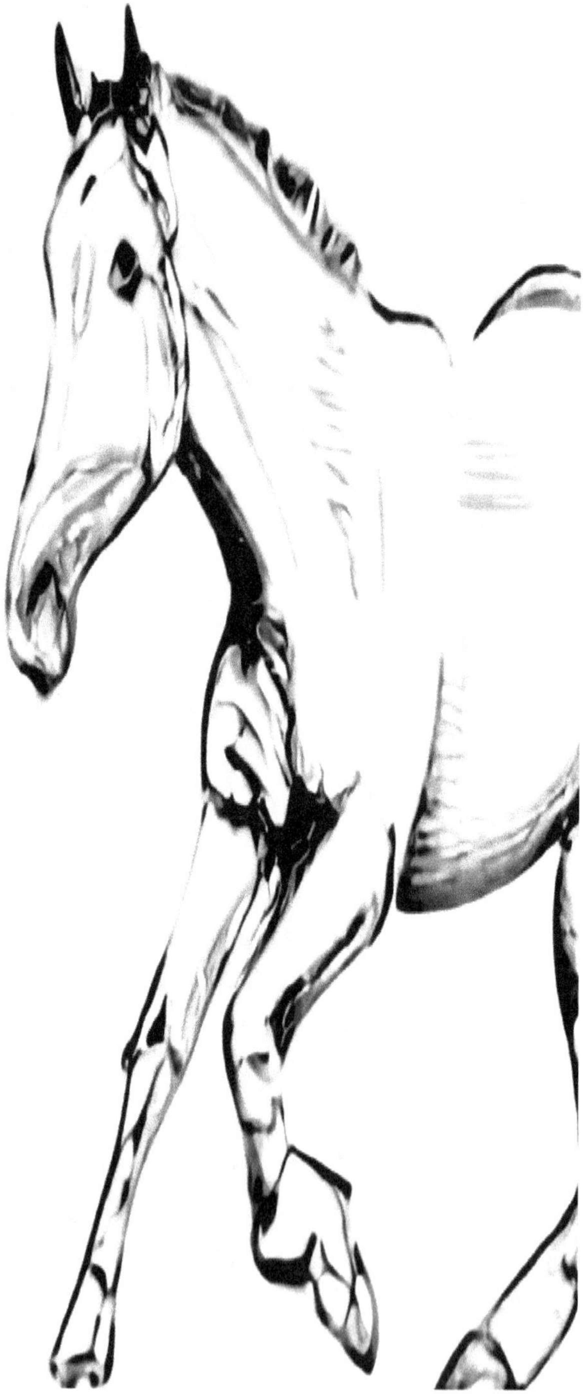

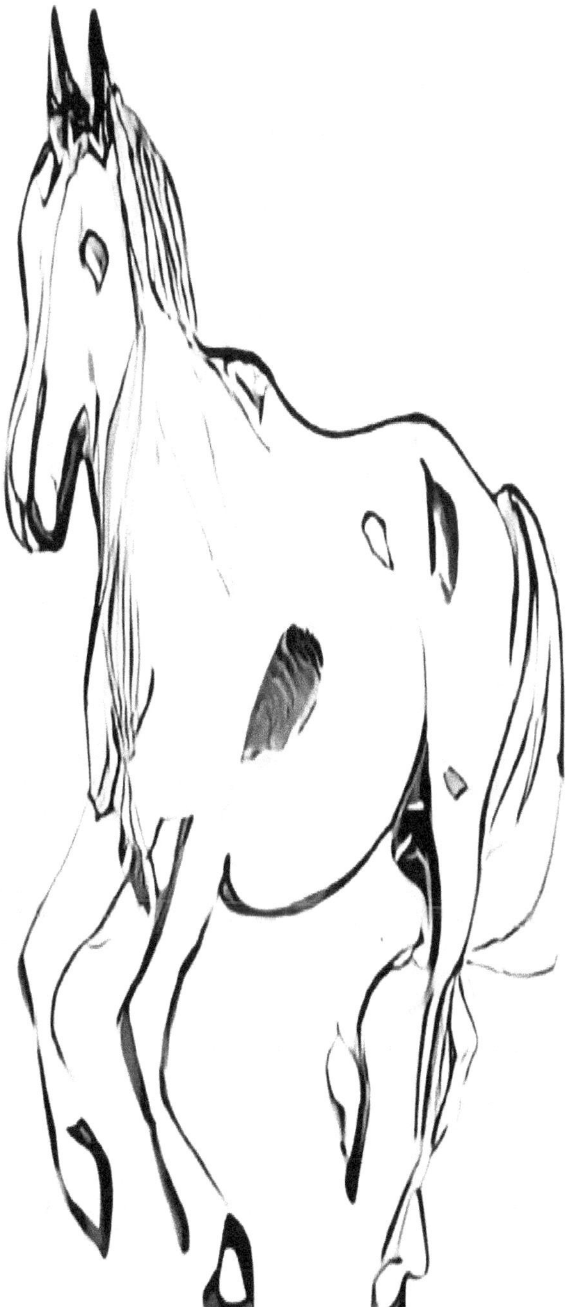

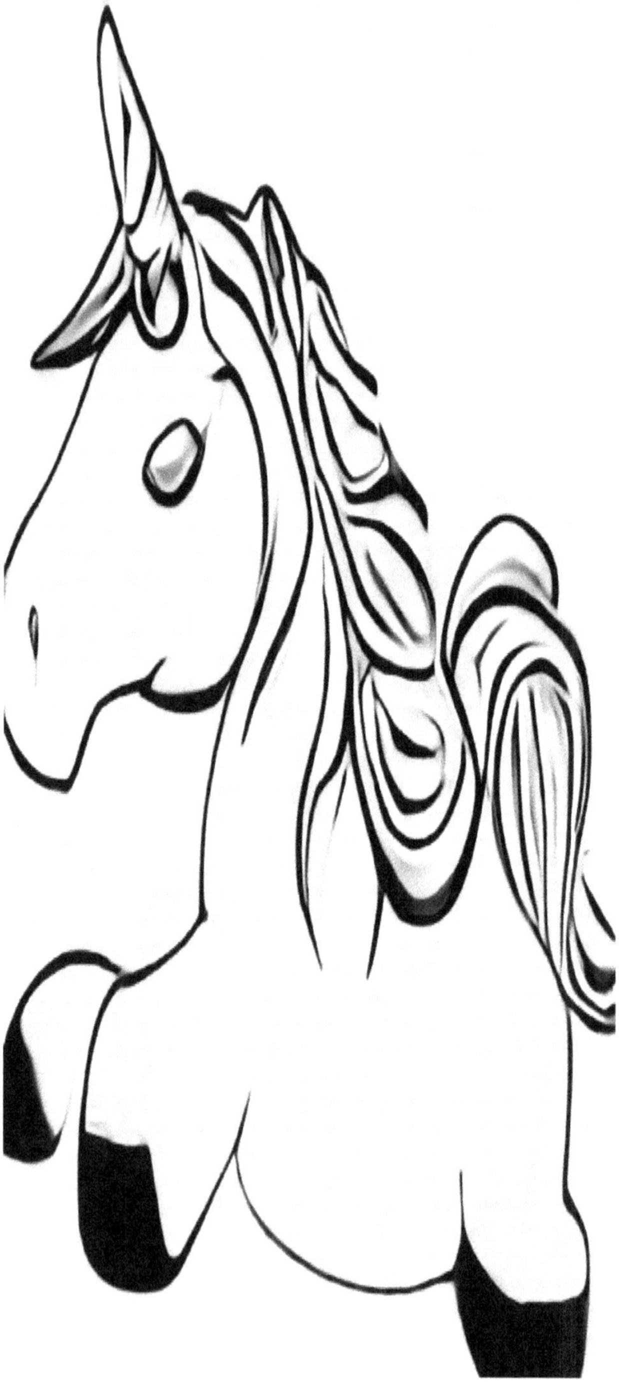

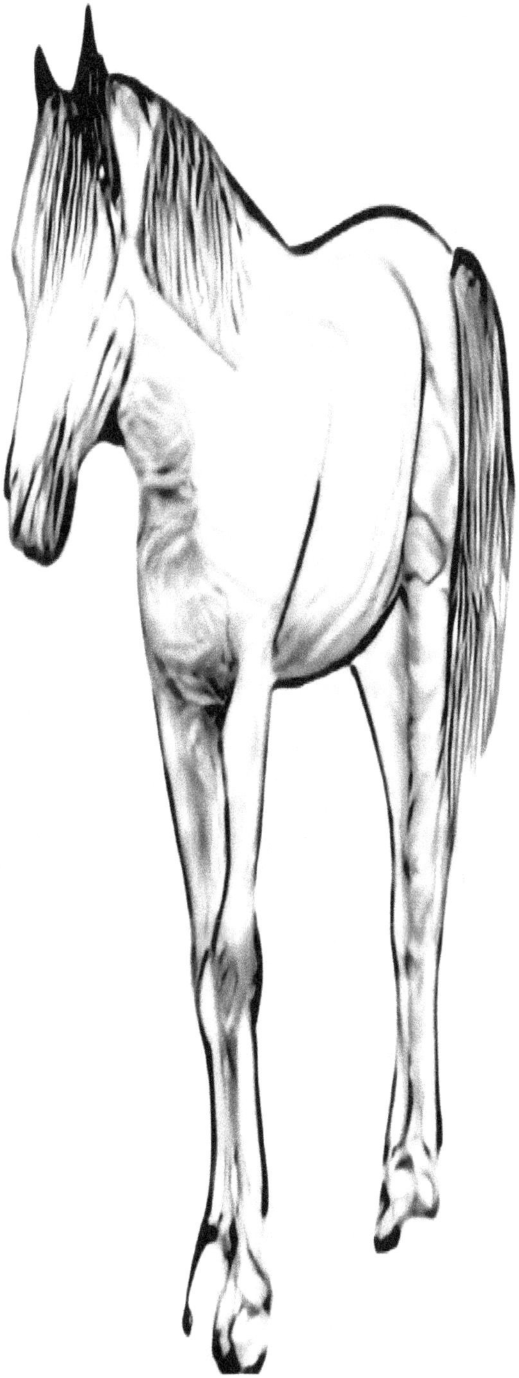

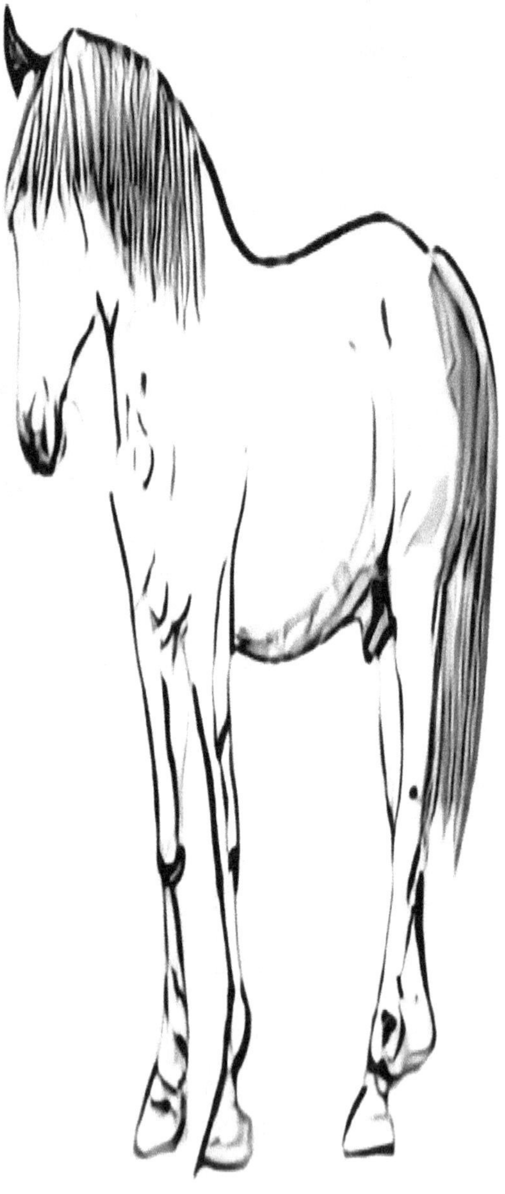

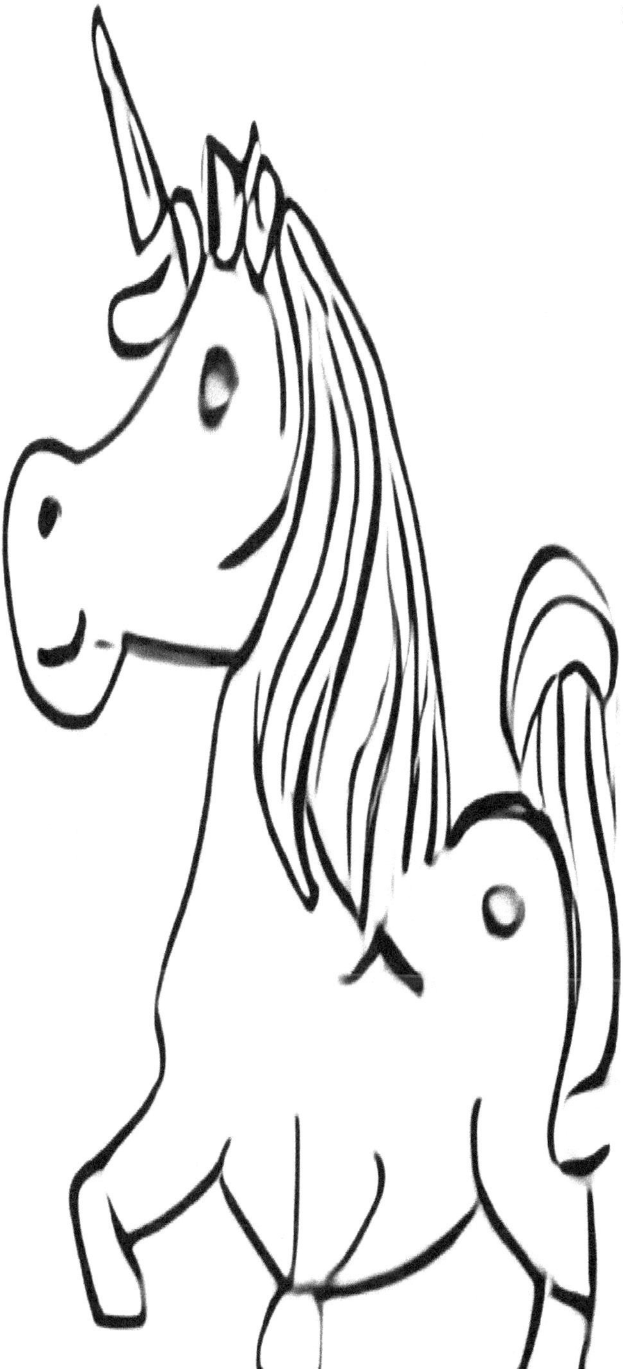

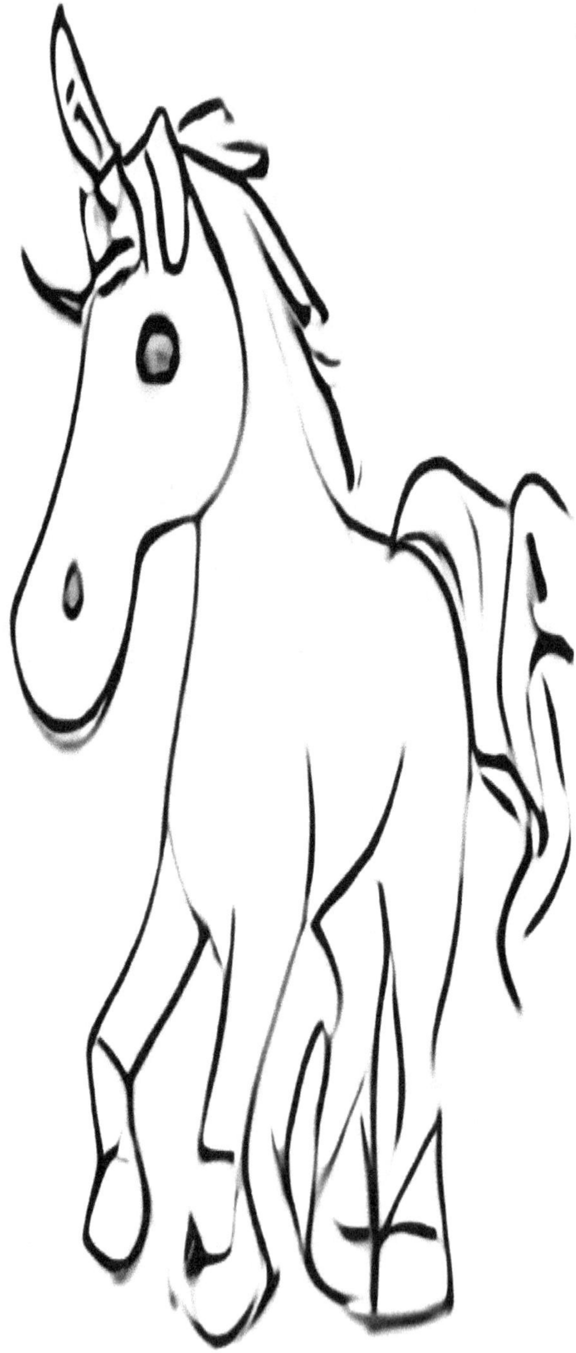

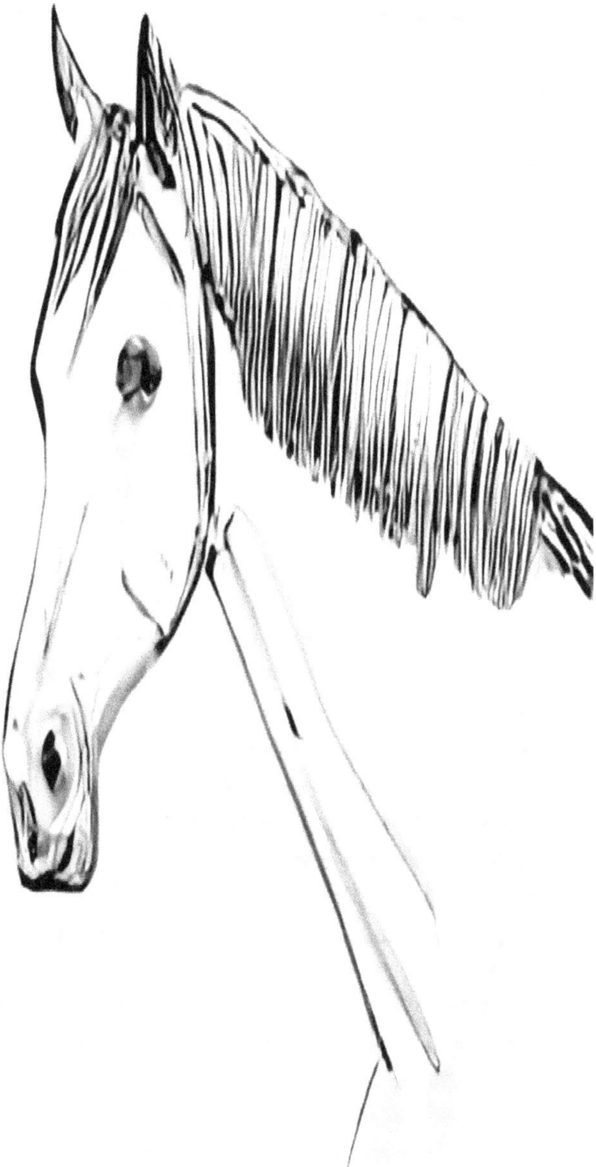

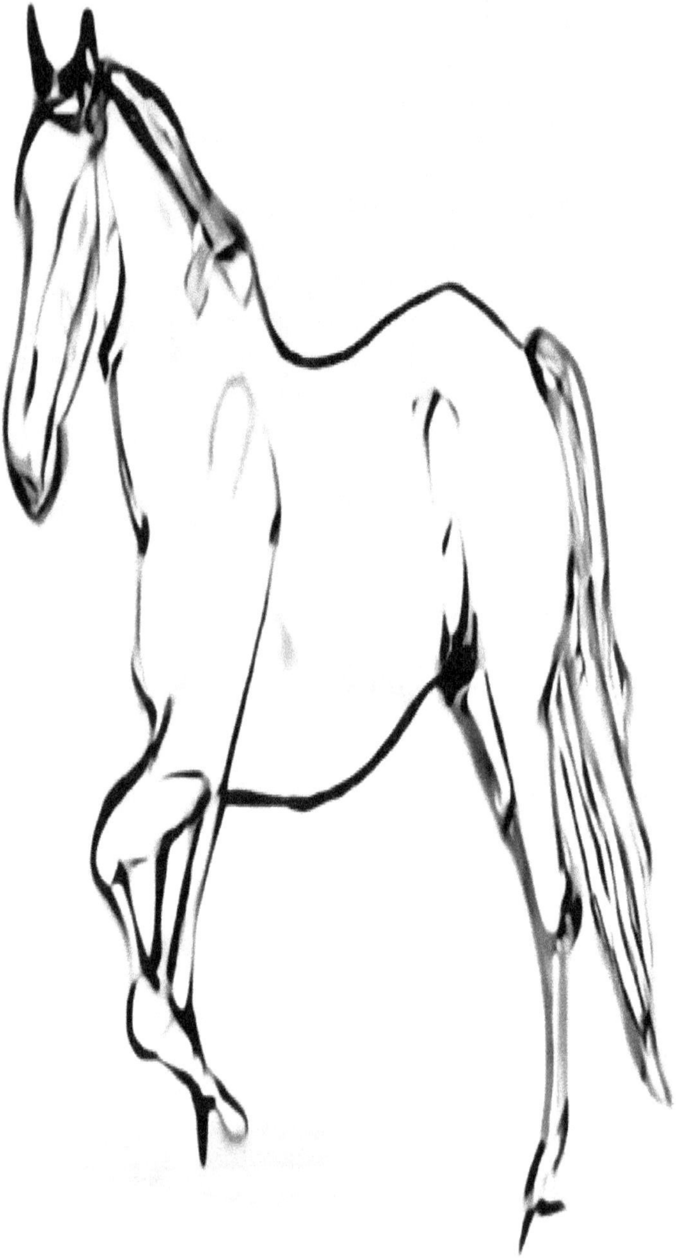

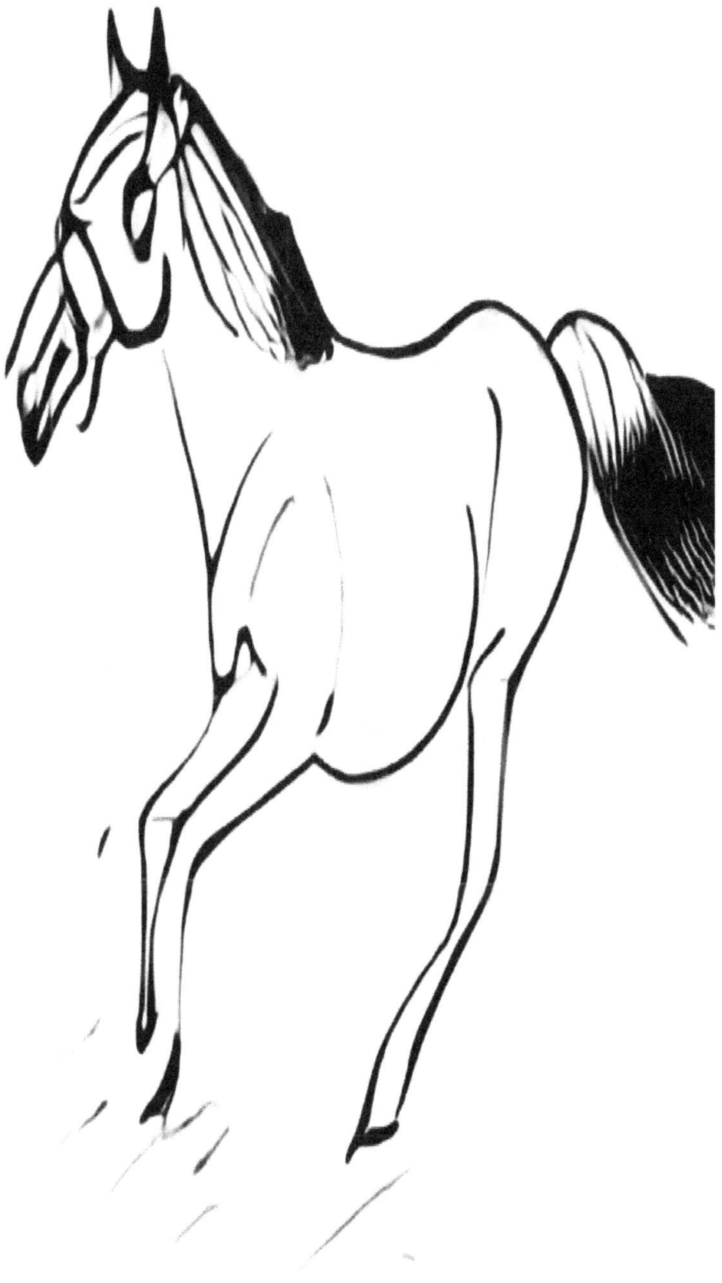

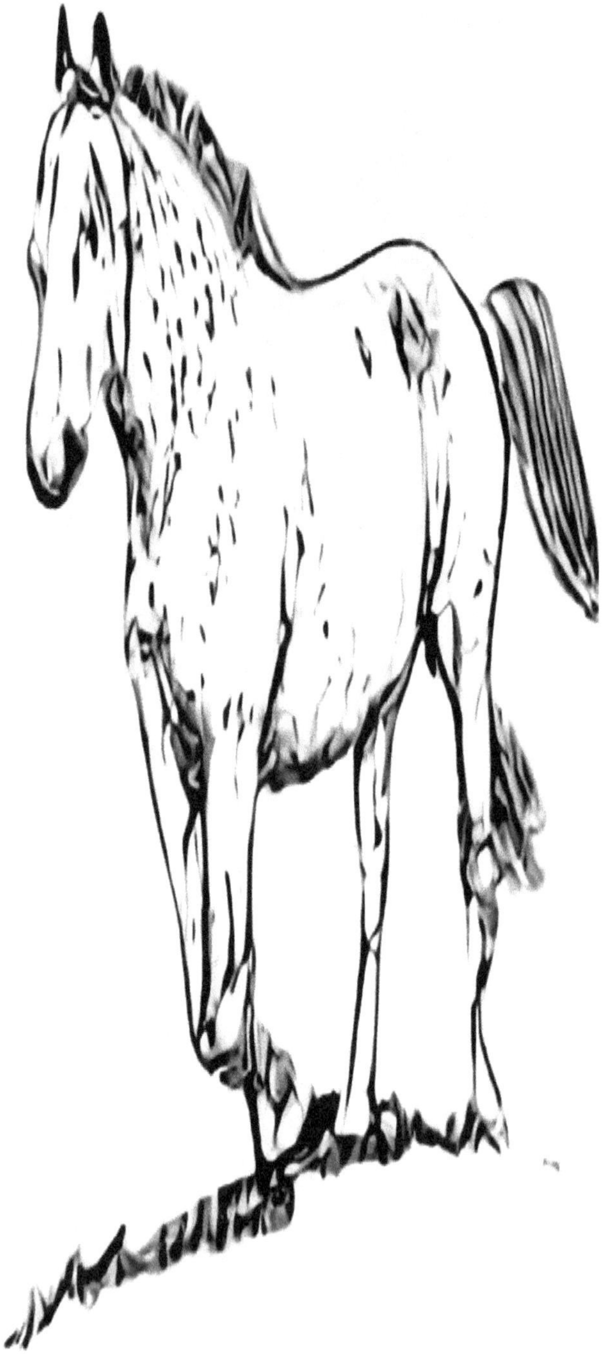

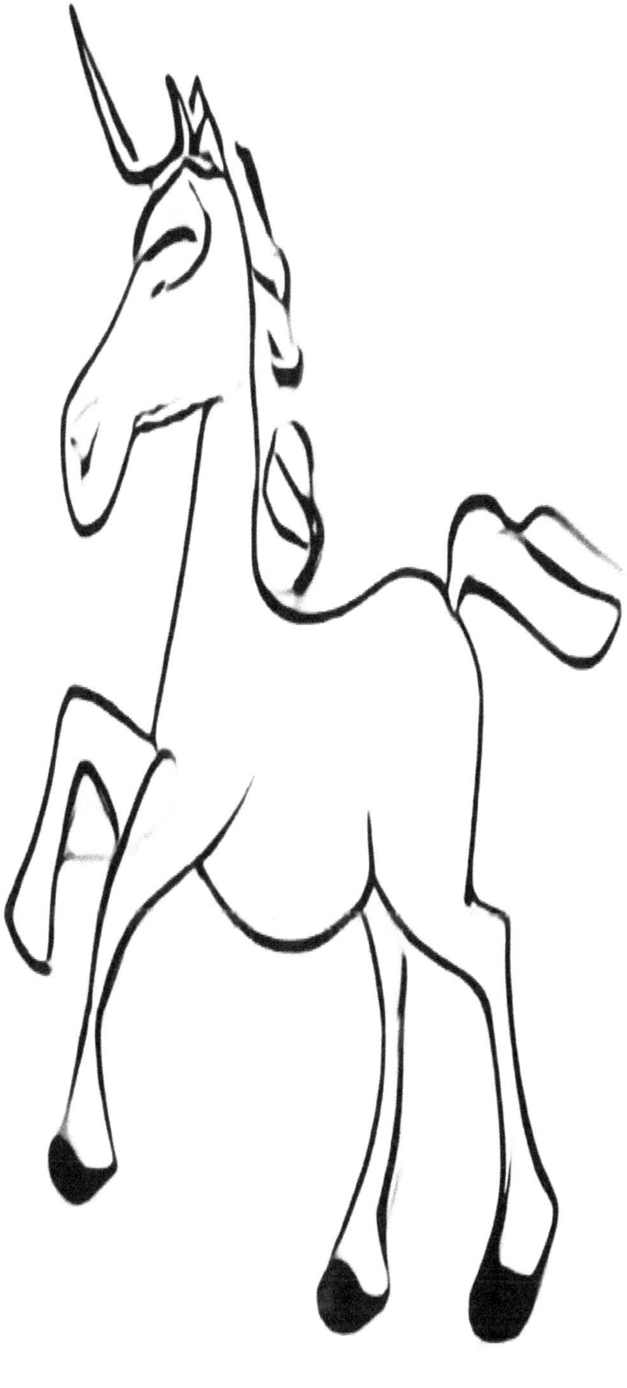

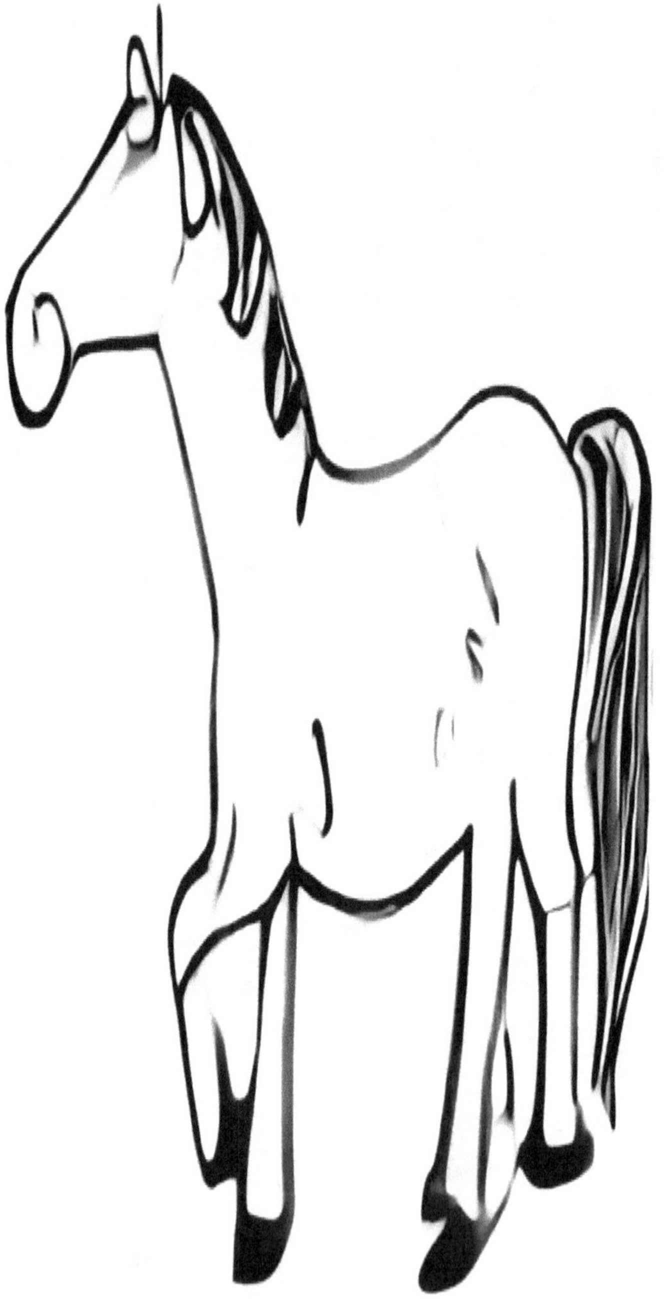

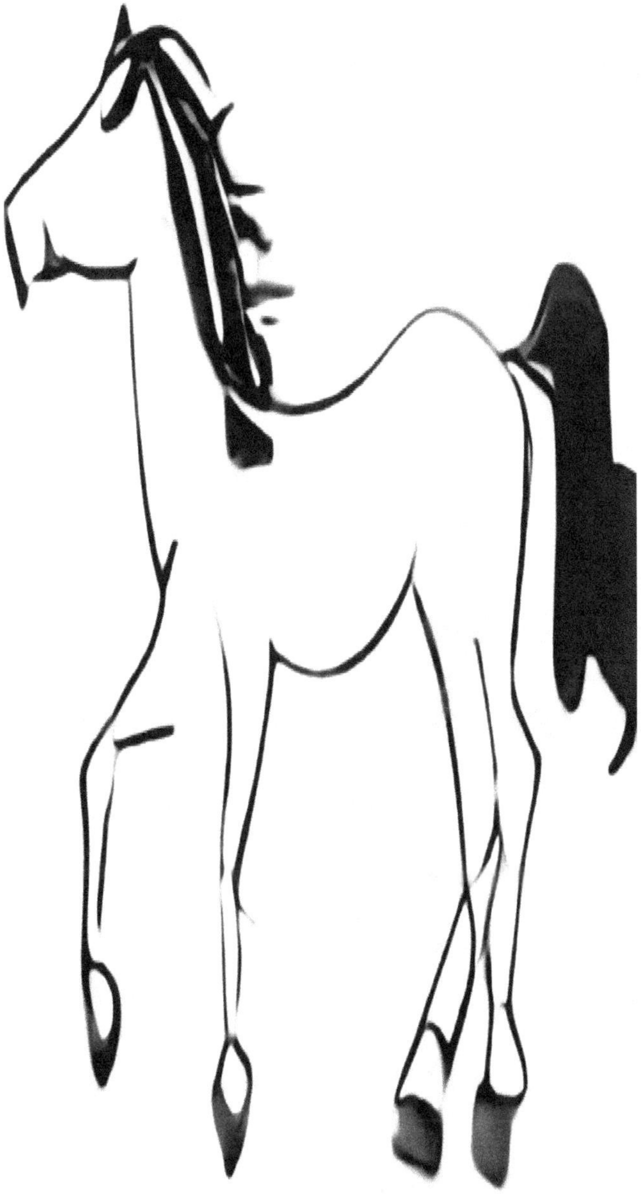

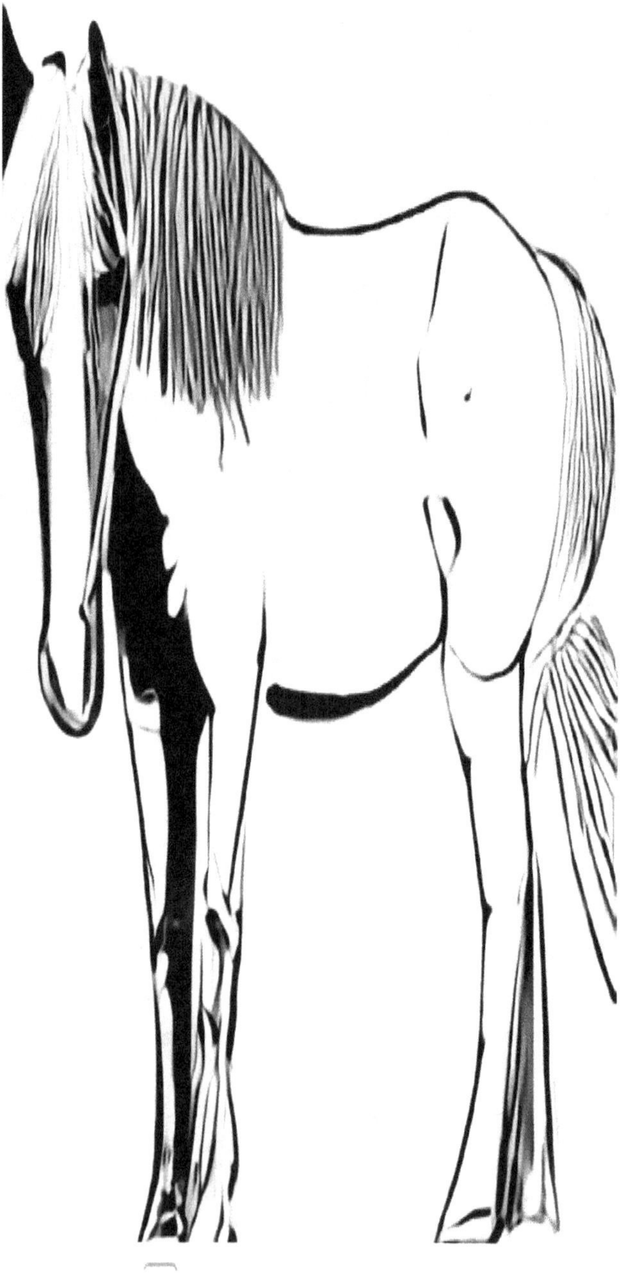

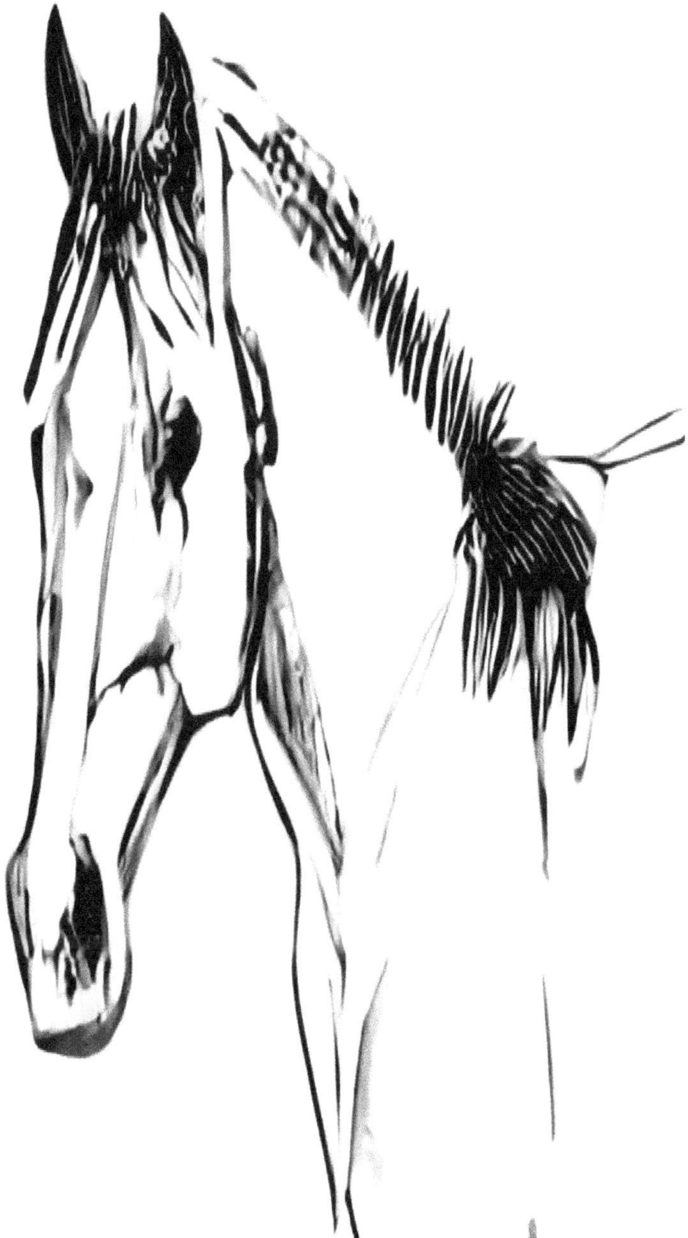

www.ingramcontent.com/pod-product-compliance
Lightning Source LLC
Chambersburg PA
CBHW070335240526
45466CB00027B/1989
* 9 7 9 8 3 9 7 9 9 0 8 0 6 *